J
796.357
Are   Aretha, David

        Power in pin-
        stripes

DUE DATE

SENSATIONAL SPORTS TEAMS

Power in Pinstripes
THE NEW YORK YANKEES

David Aretha

MyReportLinks.com Books

an imprint of

Enslow Publishers, Inc. E

Box 398, 40 Industrial Road
Berkeley Heights, NJ 07922
USA

MyReportLinks.com Books, an imprint of Enslow Publishers, Inc. MyReportLinks®
is a registered trademark of Enslow Publishers, Inc.

Library of Congress Cataloging-in-Publication Data

Power in pinstripes : the New York Yankees / David Aretha.
   p. cm. — (Sensational sports teams)
Includes bibliographical references and index.
ISBN-13: 978-1-59845-044-6
ISBN-10: 1-59845-044-1
1. New York Yankees (Baseball team)—Juvenile literature. I. Title. II. Series.
GV875.N4A74 2006
796.357'64097471—dc22

                              2006015602

Printed in the United States of America

10 9 8 7 6 5 4 3 2 1

To Our Readers:
Through the purchase of this book, you and your library gain access to the Report Links that specifically
back up this book.
The Publisher will provide access to the Report Links that back up this book and will keep these Report
Links up to date on **www.myreportlinks.com** for five years from the book's first publication date.
We have done our best to make sure all Internet addresses in this book were active and appropriate when
we went to press. However, the author and the Publisher have no control over, and assume no liability
for, the material available on those Internet sites or on other Web sites they may link to.
The usage of the MyReportLinks.com Books Web site is subject to the terms and conditions stated on the
Usage Policy Statement on **www.myreportlinks.com.**
A password may be required to access the Report Links that back up this book. The password is found
on the bottom of page 4 of this book.
Any comments or suggestions can be sent by e-mail to comments@myreportlinks.com or to the address
on the back cover.

Contents

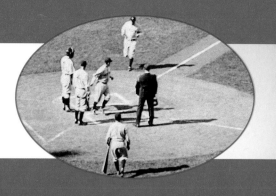

MyReportLinks.com Books
Great Books, Great Links, Great for Research!

The Internet sites featured in this book can save you hours of research time. These Internet sites—we call them **"Report Links"**—are constantly changing, but we keep them up to date on our Web site.

When you see this "Approved Web Site" logo, you will know that we are directing you to a great Internet site that will help you with your research.

Give it a try! Type http://www.myreportlinks.com into your browser, click on the series title and enter the password, then click on the book title, and scroll down to the Report Links listed for this book.

The Report Links will bring you to great source documents, photographs, and illustrations. MyReportLinks.com Books save you time, feature Report Links that are kept up to date, and make report writing easier than ever! A complete listing of the Report Links can be found on pages 114–115 at the back of the book.

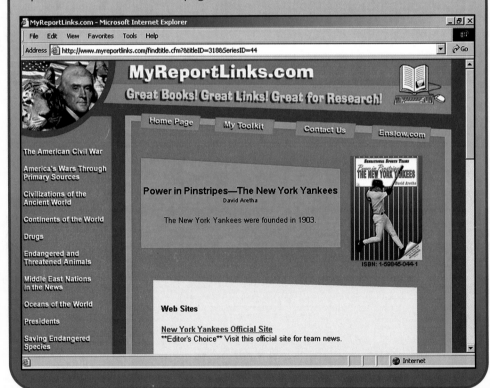

Please see "To Our Readers" on the copyright page for important information about this book, the MyReportLinks.com Web site, and the Report Links that back up this book.

Please enter NYY1597 if asked for a password.

YANKEES FACTS

➲ **Won World Series**
1923; 1927–28; 1932; 1936–39; 1941; 1943; 1947; 1949–53; 1956; 1958; 1961–62; 1977–78; 1996; 1998–2000

➲ **Won AL Pennant but Not World Series**
1921–22; 1926; 1942; 1955; 1957; 1960; 1963–64; 1976; 1981; 2001; 2003

HOME FIELD	PLAYED THERE
Oriole Park (Baltimore)	1901–02
Hilltop Park	1903–12
Polo Grounds	1913–22
Yankee Stadium	1923–73
Shea Stadium	1974–75 (while Yankee Stadium was renovated)
Yankee Stadium	1976–present
New Yankee Stadium?	2009 scheduled opening

RETIRED NUMBERS	POSITION	YEARS
No. 1: Billy Martin	Second Baseman	1950–56; 1957
	Manager	1975–79; 1983; 1985; 1988
No. 3: Babe Ruth	Right Field	1920–34
No. 4: Lou Gehrig	First Baseman	1923–39
No. 5: Joe DiMaggio	Center Fielder	1936–42; 1946–51
No. 7: Mickey Mantle	Center Fielder	1951–68
No. 8: Yogi Berra	Catcher; Left Fielder	1946–63
	Manager	1964; 1984–85
No. 8: Bill Dickey	Catcher	1928–43; 1946
No. 9: Roger Maris	Right Fielder	1960–66
No. 10: Phil Rizzuto	Shortstop	1941–42; 1946–56
No. 15: Thurman Munson	Catcher	1969–79
No. 16: Whitey Ford	Pitcher	1950; 1953–67
No. 23: Don Mattingly	First Baseman	1982–95
No. 32: Elston Howard	Catcher	1955–66; 1967
No. 37: Casey Stengel	Manager	1949–60
No. 42: Jackie Robinson*		
No. 44: Reggie Jackson	Right Fielder	1977–81
No. 49: Ron Guidry	Pitcher	1975–88

Jackie Robinson never played for the Yankees. Every team has retired his number to honor him for being the first African-American player in Major League Baseball.

These patriotic fans expressed the sentiments of many New Yorkers before Game 3 of the 2001 World Series.

RISING FROM THE ASHES

On a crisp New York night in 2001, President George W. Bush stood on the mound at Yankee Stadium prior to Game 3 of the World Series. The president donned a bulletproof vest and a sweatshirt that read "FDNY"—a tribute to the New York City Fire Department. More than fifty thousand fans stood, united. Bush looked around amid their clamor. Flashbulbs twinkled like stars, and American flags waved throughout the stands.

The president gave the crowd a supportive thumbs-up. Then, in the ceremonial first pitch, he confidently fired a strike to New York catcher Todd Greene. Again, fans roared with pride—pride for their country, pride for their city. Bush walked off the mound to chants of "USA! USA!"

Only seven weeks had passed since terrorist airplane attacks had destroyed the World Trade

Center. Approximately three thousand people were killed on September 11, and millions mourned the dead. Some New Yorkers were afraid to go to work or to step into a subway car—afraid that terrorists would strike again. Tourism in the Big Apple dropped sharply. Restaurants went out of business. New York was simply devastated— physically, financially, and emotionally.

At first, few seemed to care that the Yankees were gunning for their fourth straight World Series title. Manager Joe Torre's team made the Series, but losses at Arizona in Games 1 and 2 could not get New Yorkers out of their funk.

Even Game 3, the first Series contest at Yankee Stadium, got off to a sluggish start. Preparing for another attack, more than a thousand police offi- cers patrolled the ballpark. To enter the stadium that evening, every person—including the ballplayers—had to pass through metal detectors and have every bag checked. The lines were long and spirits were low.

Yet the president's first pitch brought a spark back to New York. Explained New York Mayor Rudy Giuliani, Bush's appearance "shows we're not afraid, we're undeterred, and that life is moving on the way it should."[1] In the midst of a very electric atmosphere, the Yankees won Game 3, 2–1, behind the gutsy pitching of Roger "The Rocket" Clemens. "He was dynamite,

dynamite!" beamed Torre.[2] The Yankees were back in business.

Because the 9/11 attacks had postponed the season by a week, Game 4 was played on Halloween. Some Yankees fans dressed in costumes, while others showed support for their team or country. In all, it was a festive, joyous night. Arizona took a 3–1 lead into the bottom of the ninth inning, but the Yankees put together one of their famous late-inning comebacks. With a man on first base and two outs, New York's Tino Martinez blasted a fly ball to center field. The ball sailed back, back and over the fence—a game-tying home run!

This site is a collection of *USA Today* sports articles covering the 2001 World Series. Coverage of each game is extensive. A photo gallery and commentaries are also included.

Access this Web site from http://www.myreportlinks.com

In the bottom of the ninth, the clock struck midnight. "Welcome to November Baseball" flashed a message on the scoreboard. Byung-Hyun Kim, a sidearm pitcher who had yielded Martinez's homer, faced Yankees shortstop Derek Jeter. Though the team's emotional spark plug, Jeter had never hit a game-ending home run in the major leagues—until now. When his slicing fly ball fell into the stands, a fan raised a sign for Jeter: "Mr. November." Jeter pumped his fist in the air as he rounded the bases, then jumped into his teammates' arms at home plate.

The next morning, all New Yorkers could talk about was their resilient reigning champions. The Yankees had won eighteen of their last twenty-one World Series games. They now needed just two wins for their fourth consecutive world title—and fifth in six years. Only two major-league teams had ever been so dominant, both of which were Yankees clubs. The 1936–39 "Bronx Bombers" won four straight world championships, and the 1949–53 Yankees took five in a row.

In Game 5, it appeared the Yankees might run out of magic. They could not touch Diamondbacks pitcher Miguel Batista, and through eight innings they trailed 2–0. But with Kim on the mound again in the ninth, New York catcher Jorge Posada socked a leadoff double, offering a glimmer of hope. Kim retired the next two batters, bringing up third baseman Scott Brosius.

Though a mediocre hitter, Brosius had often excelled in big games. In fact, he had won World Series Most Valuable Player (MVP) honors for the 1998 fall classic. This time, with the count 1–0, Brosius crushed a Kim delivery into the left-field stands. The place went wild! The Yankees, for the second straight night, had tied the game with a two-run homer with two outs in the ninth. As former Yankee Yogi Berra would have said, it was "déjà vu all over again!"

"I don't know what's going on," a bewildered Torre said afterward. "You're sitting there, you have another breath left, and Brosius hits the ball

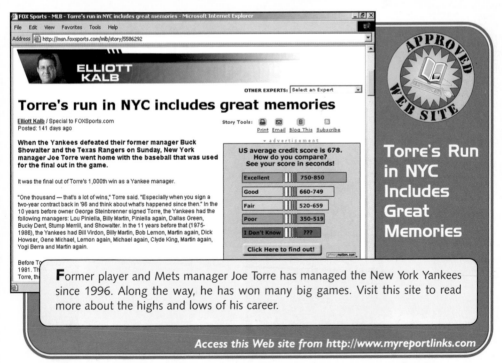

Former player and Mets manager Joe Torre has managed the New York Yankees since 1996. Along the way, he has won many big games. Visit this site to read more about the highs and lows of his career.

Access this Web site from http://www.myreportlinks.com

Derek Jeter pumps his fist to celebrate his game-winning home run that sealed Game 4 of the 2001 World Series.

out of the ballpark. I mean, you shake your head."[3]

The Yankees went on to win Game 5, 3–2, as second baseman Alfonso Soriano singled in a run in the 12th inning. Unfortunately for New York, the magical run ended in Arizona. The Diamondbacks romped in Game 6, winning 15–2. Then, while trailing 2–1 in Game 7, Arizona rallied for two runs in the ninth inning. With the score tied 2–2 and the bases loaded, slugger Luis Gonzalez blooped a single to clinch the world title.

Despite their ultimate defeat, the Yankees had achieved a higher level of success that World Series. With their three inspirational victories at Yankee Stadium, they had taught their city valuable lessons: Face the challenge. Keep hope alive. Be strong and move along.

That fall, the Yankees helped New Yorkers feel proud about their city. And yet the sentiment was nothing new. "Yankee Pride" had permeated New York for more than eighty years, since 1920, when a man named Babe Ruth first rolled into town.

Babe Ruth was a larger-than-life character who changed the fortunes of the Yankees franchise. Known as the Sultan of Swing, Ruth takes a mighty cut in this 1929 photo.

THE TEAM THAT RUTH BUILT

2

It is hard to believe, but the mighty New York Yankees were once the "Bad News Bears" of baseball. The franchise was not one of the original American League teams in 1901. It did not join the league until 1903, and it did so under the most humbling of circumstances.

On January 9, 1903, Frank Farrell and Bill Devery purchased the Baltimore Orioles for eighteen thousand dollars (which is what current star Alex Rodriguez earns per inning). The owners planned to move the team that year to the New York borough of Manhattan. Unfortunately, the club did not have a ballpark to play in.

Hundreds of workers rushed to build Hilltop Park in time for the 1903 season. The stands were simple—built of wood on a stone foundation—and accommodated fewer than 4,200 people. The playing field was enormous—542 feet from home plate to the center-field fence. The texture of the outfield resembled the moon, with rocks, baked earth, and unintentional valleys. Players called the depression in right field "Keeler's Hollow." That is where the team's best player, five-foot, four-inch Wee Willie Keeler, tried not to trip.

The ballclub was so hastily put together that it did not even have a name. Players wore black uniforms with the white letters NY across their chests. During the 1903 season, sportswriters volunteered their own names for the team: Hilltoppers, Americans, Greater New Yorks, Kilties, and Invaders. Highlanders became the most popular choice, although in 1904 the name Yankees would be bandied about.

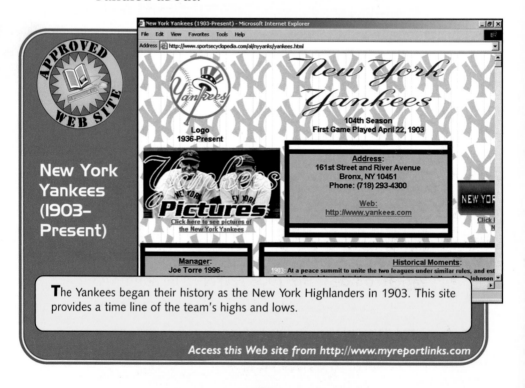

The Yankees began their history as the New York Highlanders in 1903. This site provides a time line of the team's highs and lows.

Access this Web site from http://www.myreportlinks.com

On April 22, 1903, on a cold and gray day in Washington, D.C., New York lost its very first game 3–1. It was a fitting beginning, for the team would fail to win the American League title in its first eighteen years of existence. The club hit rock bottom in 1912, finishing fifty-five games behind the Boston Red Sox. However, the team that we are now familiar with began to take shape that season. Players began to wear the famous pin-striped uniforms in 1912, and a year later the team was officially named the Yankees.

In 1913, the Yankees moved to the Polo Grounds near the Harlem River. It was a grand ballpark with thirty-four thousand seats— although the Yankees had to share it with the National League's New York Giants. In 1915, Jacob Ruppert and Colonel Tillinghast L'Hommedieu Huston purchased the Yankees for $1.25 million. It was a hefty price at the time, but in a few short years the value of the team would skyrocket.

A Man Named Babe

Yankees owner Jacob Ruppert had money to burn. He employed a butler, cook, maid, and valet to cater to his needs. He collected fine art and racehorses, and as Yankees owner, he coveted a "thoroughbred" ballplayer on the Boston Red Sox: George Herman "Babe" Ruth.

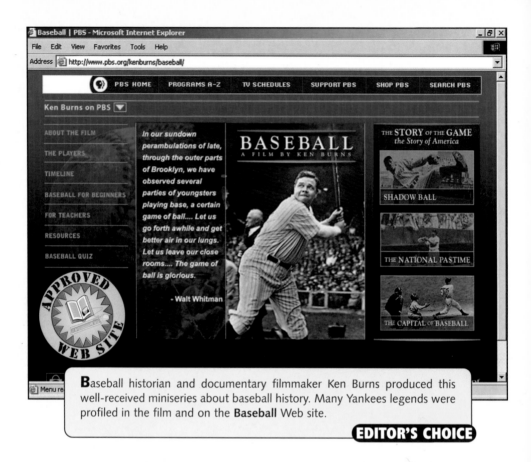

Baseball | PBS - Microsoft Internet Explorer

File   Edit   View   Favorites   Tools   Help

Address http://www.pbs.org/kenburns/baseball/

PBS HOME   PROGRAMS A–Z   TV SCHEDULES   SUPPORT PBS   SHOP PBS   SEARCH PBS

Ken Burns on PBS

ABOUT THE FILM

THE PLAYERS

TIMELINE

BASEBALL FOR BEGINNERS

FOR TEACHERS

RESOURCES

BASEBALL QUIZ

In our sundown perambulations of late, through the outer parts of Brooklyn, we have observed several parties of youngsters playing base, a certain game of ball.... Let us go forth awhile and get better air in our lungs. Let us leave our close rooms.... The game of ball is glorious.

- Walt Whitman

BASEBALL
A FILM BY KEN BURNS

THE STORY OF THE GAME
the Story of America

SHADOW BALL

THE NATIONAL PASTIME

THE CAPITAL OF BASEBALL

Baseball historian and documentary filmmaker Ken Burns produced this well-received miniseries about baseball history. Many Yankees legends were profiled in the film and on the **Baseball** Web site.

EDITOR'S CHOICE

As a small child in Baltimore, Ruth had been labeled "incorrigible" and was committed to the St. Mary's Industrial School for Boys. On the school's playgrounds, "The Bambino" developed into a fireballing pitcher and a thunderous hitter. Ruth made the major leagues with the Red Sox, with whom he averaged twenty wins a year from 1915 to 1918. When moved to the outfield in 1919, he blasted a major-league record 29 home runs.

Red Sox owner Harry Frazee needed money to finance theatrical plays that he wanted to produce. After the 1919 season, he made it clear that Ruth was for sale. Ruppert made an offer for the Babe that Frazee greedily accepted: cash and loans valued at more than $400,000. While Frazee's plays would become successful, the Red Sox would not recover from losing Ruth. According to superstitious Boston fans, the "Curse of the Bambino" is the reason why the Red Sox did not win a world championship during the rest of the century. As Ruth said, "They'll never build any monuments to Harry Frazee in Boston."[1]

Ruth Mania

Meanwhile, the homer-swatting Ruth became an enormous smash in New York. The Yankees not only set a team attendance record on May 16, 1920 (more than thirty-eight thousand fans), but police also had to turn away fifteen thousand people at the gates. In May and June alone, the Babe cracked 24 home runs. Sportswriter Grantland Rice raved about the "gorgeous, gargantuan arc" of his swing.[2] Ruth explained: "Once my swing starts, I can't change it or pull up on it. It's all or nothing."[3]

Ruth mania spread across the country that season. Out west, three cowboys rode from Wyoming to St. Louis to watch Ruth play the Browns. Allegedly, a fan in Washington, D.C., died of a heart attack after witnessing a Ruth home run. In

1920, the Yankees became the first team ever to draw one million fans in a season.

After crushing his record-breaking 30th home run on July 19, Ruth swatted his 50th and 51st on September 24. Raved *The New York Times:* "A crowd of 25,000 blazed into hysteria when the Mauling Monarch passed the fiftieth mark and gave the slugger a whoop and a hurrah he will never forget."[4] Ruth finished the season with 54 round-trippers.

Off the field, Ruth was reckless in his spending, partying, and even driving. (In one accident, his

BabeRuth.com lets you find out almost everything you would want to know about baseball legend George Herman "Babe" Ruth.

EDITOR'S CHOICE

wife flew out the window.) His antics frustrated fussy manager Miller Huggins, but the team's performance did not suffer. In 1921, Ruth belted 59 home runs, leading the Yankees to their first American League pennant (championship). That fall and in 1922, the Yankees lost the World Series to their fellow Polo Grounds occupants, the New York Giants.

The Yankees dynasty unofficially began in 1923. The team built a grand ballpark in the borough of the Bronx, called Yankee Stadium. On April 18, Ruth christened the new park with an Opening Day home run in front of 74,200 fans. The Babe that year hit .393, ripping 41 homers and drawing 170 walks. The Yanks again faced the Giants in the World Series, and this time they prevailed, winning the best-of-seven affair in six games.

Five O'Clock Lightning

The Yankees returned to the World Series in 1926 but lost to the St. Louis Cardinals. A year later, however, they annihilated the competition. The 1927 lineup was nicknamed "Murderers' Row" and "Five O'Clock Lightning" (for its explosiveness around that time in the afternoon). Ruth blasted 60 home runs that season, a record that would stand for thirty-four years. But others contributed mightily, too.

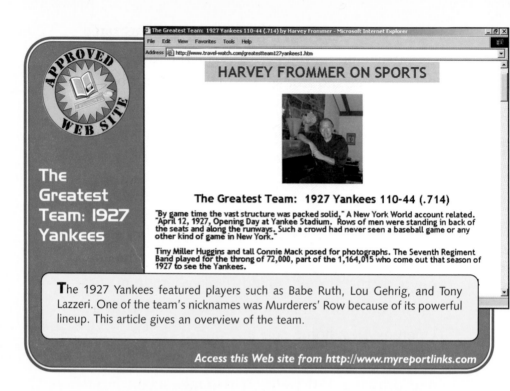

HARVEY FROMMER ON SPORTS

The Greatest Team: 1927 Yankees 110-44 (.714)

"By game time the vast structure was packed solid," A New York World account related. "April 12, 1927, Opening Day at Yankee Stadium. Rows of men were standing in back of the seats and along the runways. Such a crowd had never seen a baseball game or any other kind of game in New York."

Tiny Miller Huggins and tall Connie Mack posed for photographs. The Seventh Regiment Band played for the throng of 72,000, part of the 1,164,015 who come out that season of 1927 to see the Yankees.

The 1927 Yankees featured players such as Babe Ruth, Lou Gehrig, and Tony Lazzeri. One of the team's nicknames was Murderers' Row because of its powerful lineup. This article gives an overview of the team.

Access this Web site from http://www.myreportlinks.com

The
Greatest
Team: 1927
Yankees

First baseman Lou Gehrig emerged with a .373 average, 47 homers, and 175 runs batted in (RBI). Leadoff man Earle Combs ripped 231 hits, including 23 triples. Outfielder Bob Meusel and second baseman Tony "Push 'Em Up" Lazzeri also exceeded 100 RBIs. Behind pitching ace Waite Hoyt, the Yankees allowed the fewest runs in the league. Manager Huggins demanded smart, focused, disciplined play, and his team obliged.

Entering a Fourth of July doubleheader against Washington, New York led the Senators by nine and a half games. The Yankees proceeded to launch a fireworks show with their bats alone. The Bronx Bombers won the first game 12–1 and the second 21–1. "Those fellows not only beat you, but they tear your heart out," groaned Senators first baseman Joe Judge after the game. "I wish the season was over."[5]

The Yankees belted a major-league record 158 home runs in 1927, 102 more than any other team in the American League. They outscored their opponents 975–599, and their 110 wins set an AL record. The Pittsburgh Pirates did not stand a chance in the World Series. The Yankees swept them in four games, with the Babe tacking on two more home runs. Most historians agree that the 1927 Yankees are the greatest team in baseball history. New York continued its dominance in 1928, winning 101 games and sweeping St. Louis in the World Series.

Depression and Elation

In 1929, the Yankees became the first major-league team to make numbers a permanent part of their uniforms. Ruth and Gehrig wore No. 3 and 4, respectively, because they batted third and fourth in the lineup. The innovation, however, was a trivial footnote to a devastating season. The Yankees finished in second place, and manager Miller Huggins died of a skin disease on September 25. On October 29, the stock market crashed, plunging the United States into an economic depression that would last through much of the 1930s.

The Philadelphia Athletics won the American League pennant from 1929 through 1931. But thereafter, money problems plagued the Athletics and other AL teams—except the Yankees. Due to a large local populace and such gate attractions as Ruth and Gehrig, the Yanks remained lucrative. The 1932 Yankees, behind whip-cracking manager Joe McCarthy, won 107 games and toyed with the Chicago Cubs in the World Series.

Yankees and Cubs players hurled insults at each other during the 1932 Series, and in Game 3, Cubs fans chucked lemons at Ruth during batting practice. The Babe got revenge in the first inning,

▲ *Many baseball fans believed that Babe Ruth called his shot before hitting a home run in the 1932 World Series. Here, Ruth is rounding the bases during that home run trot. Yankees Joe Sewell and Earle Combs also scored on the round-tripper.*

belting a tremendous home run. With the score 4–4 in the fifth, Ruth stepped into the batter's box and pointed his finger toward center field. Some observers believed he was "calling his shot"—that is, predicting he would belt the next pitch over the center-field fence. He did just that, launching a 435-foot bomb into Wrigley Field's bleachers.

Ruth shared a laugh with Gehrig as he reached home plate, and Gehrig responded with a home run on the next pitch. The Yankees swept the Series, and Ruth's "Called Shot" entered baseball lore.

Four in a Row

The Babe played only two more seasons with New York (1933–34) and another with the Boston Braves. He retired with 714 career home runs, 669 as a Yankee. The Bronx Bombers, however, still had plenty of firepower. In fact, beginning in 1936, McCarthy led the Yankees to four straight world titles.

From 1936 to 1939, the Yankees won 102, 102, 99, and 106 games. Joe DiMaggio, a graceful yet powerful outfielder, emerged with a .346 average and 46 homers in 1937. Gehrig amassed 311 RBIs in 1936–37, and catcher Bill Dickey ripped .363 in 1936. Yankees pitchers led the league in ERA all four seasons, with Red Ruffing winning twenty games in each. In World Series action, New York went 16–3, outscoring their NL opponents 113–52.

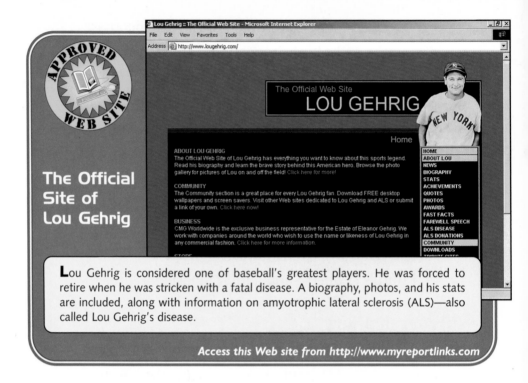

The Official
Site of
Lou Gehrig

The Official Web Site

LOU GEHRIG

NEW YORK

Home

ABOUT LOU GEHRIG
The Official Web Site of Lou Gehrig has everything you want to know about this sports legend.
Read his biography and learn the brave story behind this American hero. Browse the photo
gallery for pictures of Lou on and off the field! Click here for more!

COMMUNITY
The Community section is a great place for every Lou Gehrig fan. Download FREE desktop
wallpapers and screen savers. Visit other Web sites dedicated to Lou Gehrig and ALS or submit
a link of your own. Click here now!

BUSINESS
CMG Worldwide is the exclusive business representative for the Estate of Eleanor Gehrig. We
work with companies around the world who wish to use the name or likeness of Lou Gehrig in
any commercial fashion. Click here for more information.

STORE

HOME
ABOUT LOU
NEWS
BIOGRAPHY
STATS
ACHIEVEMENTS
QUOTES
PHOTOS
AWARDS
FAST FACTS
FAREWELL SPEECH
ALS DISEASE
ALS DONATIONS
COMMUNITY
DOWNLOADS
TRIBUTE GIFTS

Lou Gehrig is considered one of baseball's greatest players. He was forced to retire when he was stricken with a fatal disease. A biography, photos, and his stats are included, along with information on amyotrophic lateral sclerosis (ALS)—also called Lou Gehrig's disease.

Access this Web site from http://www.myreportlinks.com

Tragically, a debilitating illness forced Gehrig to retire in 1939. Eight games into the season, he had mustered only four hits—all weak singles. On May 2, 1939, the "Iron Horse" took himself out of the lineup, ending his fabled consecutive-games streak at 2,130. The dejected hero did not know what was wrong with him, claiming only that he "was no good to the club, myself, the game, or the fans."[6]

On June 19, Gehrig's thirty-sixth birthday, his doctors gave him the diagnosis. He suffered from amyotrophic lateral sclerosis, a crippling, terminal disease of the central nervous system that many still call Lou Gehrig's Disease. On July 4, the retired slugger spoke before 61,808 fans at Yankee Stadium on Lou Gehrig Day.

"Fans, for the past two weeks you have been reading about the bad break I got," Gehrig told the crowd. "Yet today I consider myself the luckiest man on the face of this earth. . . . I may have had a tough break, but I have an awful lot to live for."[7]

Babe Ruth had been estranged from Gehrig for years. But on this day, the teary legend gave Gehrig a hearty hug. Two years later, Lou Gehrig passed away.

Joltin' Joe and The Streak

Through May 15, 1941, both the Yankees and star center fielder Joe DiMaggio were off to a sluggish start. But with a hit against the White Sox that afternoon, DiMaggio sparked an extraordinary streak of greatness—for himself and the team.

Day after day, the "Yankee Clipper" continued to rip base hits. On June 17, he became the first Yankee to collect a hit in 30 consecutive games. Each morning, fans across the country checked the newspapers to see if "Joltin' Joe" had extended the streak. On July 2, he homered against the Red Sox to stretch the streak to 45 games, breaking Wee Willie Keeler's major-league record.

"The Streak" captivated the nation. DiMaggio was deluged with fan mail, and a riot nearly erupted one night as he was mobbed by autograph

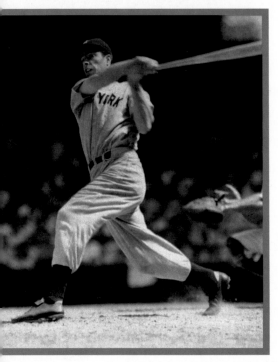

During the 1941 baseball season, Joe DiMaggio set an all-time record when he got a hit in 56 straight games. Here, Joltin Joe is shown hitting a single against the Washington Senators that season. It was the forty-second game of the streak.

seekers. DiMaggio pushed the streak past 50, yet somehow he kept his cool. "To look at Joe," recalled Yankees pitcher Lefty Gomez, "you'd never think he had any pressure on him. I never saw a guy so calm. I wound up with the upset stomachs."[8]

DiMaggio extended the record to 56 games. The streak did not end until the next game on July 17, when Cleveland third baseman Ken Keltner stymied him with two great defensive plays. Joe's red-hot hitting ignited the Yankees, who went 41–6 over a six-week stretch. After they won the World Series over the Brooklyn Dodgers, DiMaggio was named league MVP.

Off to War

On December 7, 1941, the Japanese attacked Pearl Harbor, Hawaii, triggering America's entry into World War II. President Franklin Roosevelt ruled that major-league baseball could continue

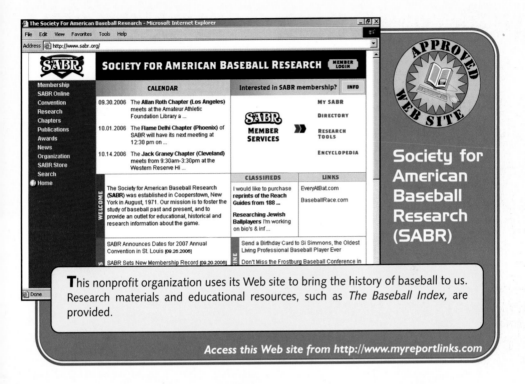

This nonprofit organization uses its Web site to bring the history of baseball to us. Research materials and educational resources, such as *The Baseball Index*, are provided.

Access this Web site from http://www.myreportlinks.com

during the war. The game went on, but many of the sport's stars enlisted in the military. DiMaggio, shortstop Phil Rizzuto, and pitcher Red Ruffing were among the Yankees who traded pinstripes for Army fatigues. Taking their places were such forgottens as Snuffy Stirnweiss and Oscar Grimes.

Although the Bombers won the World Series in 1943, fans were too preoccupied to celebrate. But in 1945, after the Allies' victories in Europe and Japan, Americans finally breathed a collective sigh of relief. The war was over, and it was time to enjoy life—including the national pastime. In 1946, New Yorkers would flock to Yankee Stadium in record numbers.

▲ Yankee great Lawrence "Yogi" Berra (center) is flanked by his teammates Elston Howard (left) and Johnny Blanchard (right). This photo was taken in 1963.

FROM YOGI TO REGGIE

3

With the war over, the stars came back to big-league parks in 1946—and so did the fans. In fact, huge crowds turned out for Yankees preseason games, and not just to croon over hero Joe DiMaggio. "[I]t wasn't Joe they were cheering," wrote sportswriter Red Smith. "It was the return of big league baseball."[1] At Yankee Stadium in 1946, 2,265,512 people spun through the turnstiles, smashing the major-league record.

The Red Sox won the American League pennant in 1946, but the Yankees got revenge a year later. They outscored Boston 40–5 in one regular-season series and roared to the World Series. The 1947 Yankees boasted the best pitching in the league as well as a talented rookie catcher. Yogi Berra looked and talked kind of funny, but boy could he play. "So I'm ugly," Berra once said. "So what? I never saw anyone hit with his face."[2] In Game 4 of the World Series against Brooklyn, Yankees pitcher Bill Bevins lost a no-hitter and the game with two outs in the ninth. Still, the Yankees took the Series in seven games.

On August 16, 1948, after battling throat cancer, Babe Ruth died at age fifty-three. The nation grieved the passing of one of its greatest heroes. As Ruth's body lay in state at Yankee Stadium, with the flag at half-mast, more than one hundred thousand mourners filed past his casket. Little Leaguers came in uniform, and vendors sold hot dogs—the Babe's favorite snack.

In the last twenty-eight years of Ruth's life, the Yankees had won eleven world titles. Little did anyone realize that even greater days lay ahead.

High Five

When the Yankees hired Casey Stengel as manager for the 1949 season, reporters scratched their heads. Not only did the new skipper possess a managerial record of 581–742, but he also talked nonsensically. Dave Egan of the *Boston Record* mimicked "Stengelese" when commenting on his signing: "Well, sirs and ladies, the Yankees have now been mathematically eliminated from the 1949 pennant race. They eliminated themselves when they engaged Perfesser Casey Stengel to mismanage them for the next two years. . . ."[3]

Despite his twisted English, Stengel owned a brilliant baseball mind. Stengel brought a platoon system to the Yankees. His strategy, wrote Paul Adomites, was to "put each player in a situation where he is most likely to succeed."[4] For example, if a player could not hit hard fastballs, he would not play against fireballers.

Maximizing the Yankees' talent, Stengel won world championships in his first five seasons with the team. Berra was the backbone of the ballclub, winning the AL MVP Award in 1951. Phil Rizzuto copped the award in 1950, hitting .324 and providing stellar defense at shortstop. Pitchers Vic Raschi, Ed Lopat, and Allie Reynolds all enjoyed

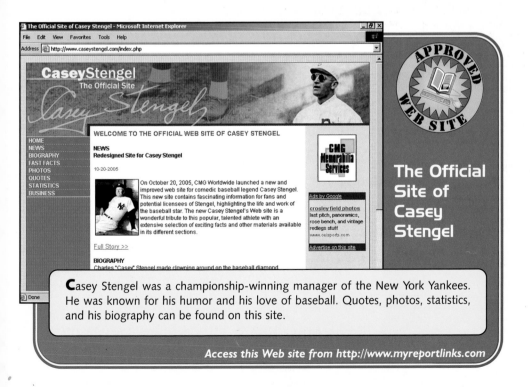

Casey Stengel was a championship-winning manager of the New York Yankees. He was known for his humor and his love of baseball. Quotes, photos, statistics, and his biography can be found on this site.

Access this Web site from http://www.myreportlinks.com

twenty-win seasons. And in 1951, rookie Mickey Mantle joined the team. Mantle, claimed Stengel, "had more speed than any slugger and more slug than any speedster."[5]

None of the 1949–53 teams won one hundred games. But since Stengel used so many players during each season, he was able to keep stars fresh while also playing "hot hands" during the World Series. As a result, the Yankees defeated the Philadelphia Phillies, New York Giants, and the Brooklyn Dodgers (three times) in the World Series. Only one Series went seven games. "Five straight world championships ain't a bad record at all," boasted Stengel.[6] In fact, no other team in history has achieved the feat.

Approaching Perfection

In 1955, the Yankees made it back to the World Series, where Brooklyn finally beat them. The following season, however, the Bombers would not be denied. Two players—a superstar slugger and a mediocre pitcher—made 1956 a season to remember.

Mickey Mantle, the greatest switch-hitter of all time, peaked in 1956. On May 30, he came within 18 inches of belting a ball clear out of Yankee Stadium—something no one has ever done. Some have estimated that the ball would have traveled 600 feet. "The Mick" that season won the Triple

▲ *Catcher Yogi Berra (No. 8) leaps into the arms of pitcher Don Larsen after they recorded the final out of Larsen's perfect game during the 1956 World Series.*

Crown, leading the league in batting average (.353), home runs (52), and RBIs (130). He added three more homers in the World Series against Brooklyn.

The Series, though, belonged to Don Larsen. A hulking, slouched-shouldered pitcher, Larsen had trouble throwing strikes in 1956. As the starter in Game 5, however, he threw with surgical precision. Through eight innings, he owned a perfect game. That means he retired every batter he had faced—no hits, no walks, no men on base. No one had ever pitched a no-hitter in the World Series before, let alone a perfect game.

With one out in the ninth inning, Roy Campanella blasted a Larsen pitch just foul. "I was so nervous, I almost fell down," Larsen recalled. "My legs were rubbery, and my fingers didn't feel like they were on my hand. I said to myself, 'Please help me out, somebody.'"[7]

Campanella grounded out, and then Larsen struck out Dale Mitchell for the final stroke of his masterpiece. Catcher Yogi Berra jumped into his pitcher's arms, while sixty-four thousand fans at Yankee Stadium roared in delight. Afterward, a reporter asked Larsen, "Is that the best game you ever pitched?"[8] An answer was not necessary.

Three Series That Went the Limit

The Yankees found a new World Series rival in 1957 and 1958: the Milwaukee Braves, led by

Hank Aaron (who would break Babe Ruth's record of 714 career home runs in 1974). Both Series lasted the full seven games. The Braves won Game 7 in 1957 on Lew Burdette's shutout. New York responded with a Game 7 triumph in 1958 thanks to a key three-run homer by Moose Skowron.

In 1960, Casey Stengel led the Yankees to their tenth World Series in twelve years. New York was a heavy favorite against Pittsburgh, but the Pirates forced a Game 7 at Forbes Field. Though the Yankees led 7–4 in the eighth inning, the remainder of the game was a roller-coaster ride. Pittsburgh went ahead 9–7 in the eighth, and New York tied the score at 9–9 in the ninth. Then, in the bottom of the inning, Pittsburgh's Bill

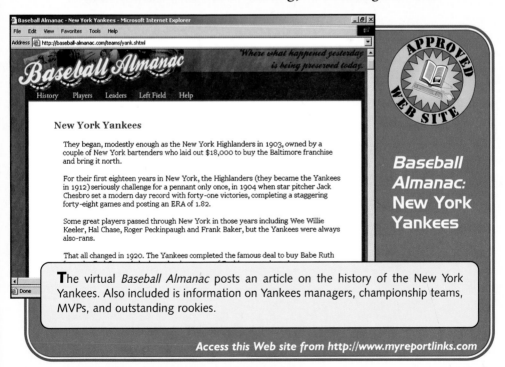

Baseball Almanac: New York Yankees

The virtual *Baseball Almanac* posts an article on the history of the New York Yankees. Also included is information on Yankees managers, championship teams, MVPs, and outstanding rookies.

Access this Web site from http://www.myreportlinks.com

Mazeroski cracked the most heartbreaking hit in Yankees history: a game-ending, series-winning home run. "I was so disappointed," said Mantle, "I cried on the plane ride home."[9]

After the Series, the Yankees fired Stengel, saying they wanted a more youthful organization. Cracked Casey: "I'll never make the mistake of being seventy again."[10]

Maris One-Ups the Babe

In 1961, Yankees outfielders Mickey Mantle and Roger Maris threatened to break Babe Ruth's major-league record for home runs in a season (60 dingers). Yet while many New Yorkers pulled for the all-American Mantle to surpass the milestone, Maris had few fans in his corner. Not a home-grown Yankee, Maris had come over in a trade from the Kansas City Athletics prior to the 1960 season. Quiet and reserved, he came off as aloof and sullen.

Both Maris and Mantle topped 50 homers by the beginning of September, but The Mick dropped out of the chase with an injury. Meanwhile, reporters pointed out that Ruth had hit his 60 in a 154-game schedule, while Maris had 162 games in 1961 to accomplish the feat. Moreover, many New Yorkers felt a greater allegiance to their beloved Ruth than Maris. "Every day I went to the ballpark in Yankee Stadium, as well as on the road, people were on my back," Maris said.[11] For Maris, the pressure to break the record—while being vilified by the media—was overwhelming. His hair was falling out in clumps.

Yet on the last day of the season, in front of a mostly empty Yankee Stadium, Maris came through. He cracked a fastball from Boston's Tracy Stallard into the right-field seats for his 61st home run. At last, fans gave him his due: a standing ovation and a curtain call. The new home run king thanked his well-wishers with a beaming smile and a gracious tip of the cap.

Dynasty in Decline

The Yankees won the 1961 AL pennant thanks to the "M&M" boys (Maris and Mantle) and crafty pitcher Whitey Ford (who posted a 25–4 record). They breezed past Cincinnati in the World Series, and they downed San Francisco in the fall classic a year later—although that Series went down to the wire. Trailing 1–0 in Game 7, the Giants put runners on second and third with two outs in the bottom of the ninth. The next batter, fearsome slugger Willie McCovey, ripped a screaming liner—right to the glove of second baseman Bobby Richardson. The Yankees won their twentieth world championship.

The Bombers copped two more pennants in 1963 and 1964, giving them twenty-nine first-place

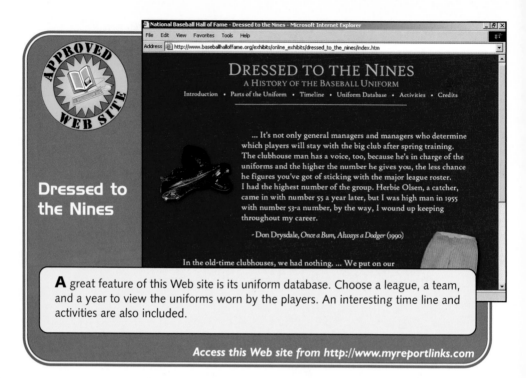

National Baseball Hall of Fame - Dressed to the Nines - Microsoft Internet Explorer

File   Edit   View   Favorites   Tools   Help

Address http://www.baseballhalloffame.org/exhibits/online_exhibits/dressed_to_the_nines/index.htm

DRESSED TO THE NINES
A HISTORY OF THE BASEBALL UNIFORM

Introduction • Parts of the Uniform • Timeline • Uniform Database • Activities • Credits

... It's not only general managers and managers who determine which players will stay with the big club after spring training. The clubhouse man has a voice, too, because he's in charge of the uniforms and the higher the number he gives you, the less chance he figures you've got of sticking with the major league roster. I had the highest number of the group. Herbie Olsen, a catcher, came in with number 55 a year later, but I was high man in 1955 with number 53-a number, by the way, I wound up keeping throughout my career.

- Don Drysdale, *Once a Bum, Always a Dodger* (1990)

In the old-time clubhouses, we had nothing. ... We put on our

Dressed to the Nines

A great feature of this Web site is its uniform database. Choose a league, a team, and a year to view the uniforms worn by the players. An interesting time line and activities are also included.

Access this Web site from http://www.myreportlinks.com

finishes over a forty-four-year span. But New York lost each World Series, first to the Los Angeles Dodgers and then to the St. Louis Cardinals. When the Columbia Broadcasting System (CBS) bought the Yankees in 1964, it was clear that the dynasty was over. Such stars as Maris, Mantle, Berra, and Ford were either gone or over the hill. Promising prospects, such as first baseman Joe Pepitone, fell short of stardom. During the next decade, managers Johnny Keane, Ralph Houk, and Bill Virdon would fail to even contend for an AL pennant.

⊜ Buying a Championship

With trips to the 1969 and 1973 World Series, the New York Mets—not the Yankees—captured the city's attention. In fact, the Bombers were guests in the Mets' Shea Stadium for two years while Yankee Stadium was being remodeled. But in 1975, the balance of power shifted thanks to bold acquisitions by new Yankees owner George Steinbrenner.

With free agency becoming a part of the game, star pitcher Catfish Hunter was available to the highest bidder. On January 1, 1975, Steinbrenner signed him to a four-year contract worth $3.75 million. Later in the year, "The Boss" signed feisty manager (and former Yankees second baseman) Billy Martin.

The Yankees moved back home in 1976 and captured the AL Eastern Division title. Catcher

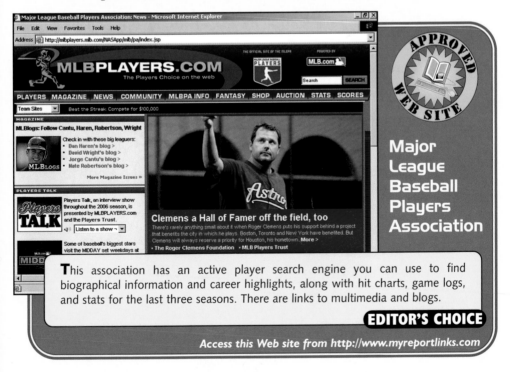

This association has an active player search engine you can use to find biographical information and career highlights, along with hit charts, game logs, and stats for the last three seasons. There are links to multimedia and blogs.

EDITOR'S CHOICE

Access this Web site from http://www.myreportlinks.com

Thurman Munson and a deep, well-paid pitching staff led the way. In the AL Championship Series against Kansas City, first baseman Chris Chambliss belted a game-ending, series-winning home run. Yankees fans mobbed their hero as he circled the bases. Although New York lost the 1976 World Series to Cincinnati, the excitement was back in the Bronx.

On the Rise

With revenue now pouring in, Steinbrenner signed another big-ticket free agent: former Oakland A's superstar outfielder Reggie Jackson. The vain but charismatic slugger reportedly called himself the "straw that stirs the drink."[12] He clashed often with his hotheaded manager, but in the 1977 World Series he delivered. In Game 6 against the Dodgers—with fans chanting "Reggie! Reggie! Reggie!"—Jackson electrified Yankee Stadium with three consecutive home runs. The Yankees that night won their first world title in fifteen years, and Jackson would forever be known as "Mr. October."

By 1978, Boston Red Sox fans were still plagued by the "Curse of the Bambino." Since selling Babe Ruth to the Yankees in 1920, Boston had won zero World Series while New York had won twenty-one. In 1973, a brawl between the two teams fueled the heated rivalry. Five years later, the Yankees frustrated the Sox to the ultimate degree.

Trailing Boston in the standings by fourteen games in the summer of 1978, the Yankees stormed back on the arm of Ron "Louisiana Lightning" Guidry. In a September series, they outscored the Red Sox by a combined score of 42–9 in what was dubbed "The Boston Massacre." Then, in a one-game playoff for the AL East title, New York beat the Red Sox, 5–4, thanks to a home run by light-hitting shortstop Bucky Dent.

In the 1978 World Series, the Yankees downed the Dodgers in six games, thanks in part to great defensive gems by third baseman Graig Nettles.

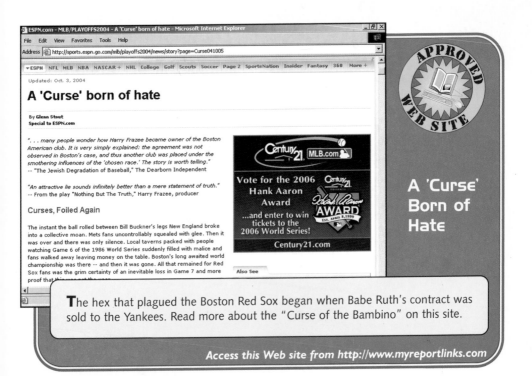

The hex that plagued the Boston Red Sox began when Babe Ruth's contract was sold to the Yankees. Read more about the "Curse of the Bambino" on this site.

Access this Web site from http://www.myreportlinks.com

Though Steinbrenner had fired manager Martin in midseason, he rehired him for the 1979 season. Through victory and controversy, The Boss's team made headlines every day. Mets fans could not deny it: The Yankees were once again kings of New York.

The Long Drought

In 1981, the Yankees signed another high-priced free agent: six-foot six-inch slugger Dave Winfield.

Although, Steinbrenner's efforts to buy happiness no longer worked. New York lost the World Series to the Dodgers in 1981, as Winfield mustered just one hit in 22 at-bats in the World Series (a .045 batting average). The Yankees did not make the playoffs over the next thirteen seasons.

◀ *Jim Abbott was born without a right hand. That did not stop him from throwing a no-hitter while playing for the Yankees in 1993.*

Yankees fans in the 1980s idolized Don Mattingly, a Gold Glove first baseman who won the AL MVP Award in 1985. And on September 4, 1993, Yankees pitcher Jim Abbott performed one of the most amazing feats in baseball history. Born without a right hand, Abbott threw a no-hitter against the Cleveland Indians.

Under thirty-eight-year-old manager Buck Showalter, the Yankees finally reemerged as a force in 1994. They went 70–43 as a first-place team, although a players-owners labor dispute forced the cancellation of the postseason. In 1995, New York made the playoffs as a wildcard team but lost to Seattle in the finale of the Division Series. That was not good enough for Steinbrenner, who replaced Showalter with veteran manager Joe Torre after the season. At that point, few would have believed that the Yankees were about to enter a long period of steady leadership—and extraordinary success.

Yankee fan Jeffrey Maier became a part of team lore when he reached over the fence and prevented Orioles outfielder Tony Tarasco from catching Derek Jeter's home run ball. Maier eventually played college baseball for Wesleyan University.

THE NEW DYNASTY

In 1996, rookie Derek Jeter brought a spark to the Yankees that they sorely needed. A slick-fielding shortstop, Jeter infused the team with positive energy, speed at the top of the lineup, and .300 hitting punch. Moreover, he electrified Yankee Stadium with his hustle and winning smile.

Jeter's enthusiasm spread throughout the entire lineup in 1996. Five starters ripped over .300, and two others hit in the .290s. First baseman Tino Martinez, who came over from Seattle, knocked in 117 runs. Center fielder Bernie Williams arose as a force, socking 29 homers. On the mound, young Andy Pettitte emerged with 21 victories. For the first time since 1981, the Yankees won the AL Eastern Division title.

In the postseason in 1996, everyone contributed—even the fans. After breezing past Texas in the AL Division Series, the Yankees opened the

AL Championship Series at home against Baltimore. In the eighth inning of Game 1, Jeter launched a fly ball to the wall in right field. Tony Tarasco appeared ready to catch it until twelve-year-old fan Jeffrey Maier stuck his glove out and knocked the ball away. The umpire ruled it a home run, and the Yankees won the game in extra innings. Yankees Mayor Rudy Giuliani declared Jeffrey a Yankees hero.

New York rolled past Baltimore in five games. Then, after dropping the first two games of the World Series, the Yankees ripped off four straight victories. Included was an extra-inning win in Game 4 and a 1–0 Pettitte triumph in Game 5. After prevailing 3–2 in Game 6, Yankees third base-man Wade Boggs trotted around Yankee Stadium on a policeman's horse. For the first time since 1978, the Yankees were World Series champions.

⊜The 125-Win Season

The Yankees won 96 games in 1997 but lost to Cleveland in the first round of the playoffs. Owner George Steinbrenner was not happy. General Manager Bob Watson was fed up with the owner and quit. In 1998, however, all of the pieces fell into place, and the frequently meddle-some owner sat back and enjoyed the season.

Through June, the Yankees were 56–20. David Cone would go on to win 20 games, while husky

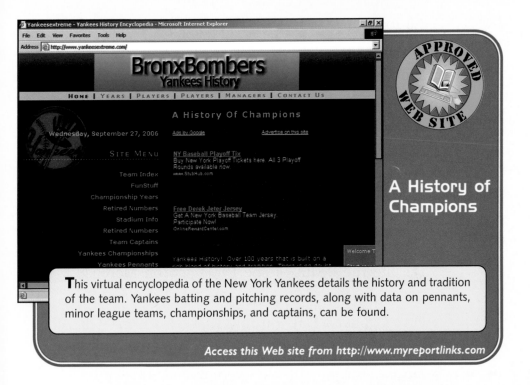

A History of
Champions

This virtual encyclopedia of the New York Yankees details the history and tradition of the team. Yankees batting and pitching records, along with data on pennants, minor league teams, championships, and captains, can be found.

Access this Web site from http://www.myreportlinks.com

David Wells pitched a perfect game on May 17. Relief ace Mariano Rivera recorded 36 saves. Offensively, the lineup was stacked with quality hitters. Jeter ripped .324 with 127 runs scored. Martinez knocked in 123 runs, while outfielder Paul O'Neill drove in 116. "We have extreme confidence regardless of what inning it is or where we are in the batting order," said Cone.[1]

Manager Joe Torre's juggernaut led the league in runs scored, ERA, and fielding percentage in 1998. They recorded 114 regular-season wins—the most in AL history. In the postseason, New York rolled over Texas, Cleveland, and San Diego, sweeping the Padres in four World Series games.

All told, the Yankees won 125 games, an all-time major-league record. Most impressively, they showed professionalism and class throughout the season. "[They] never bashed anybody's head or danced on anybody's grave," said Yankees general manager Brian Cashman. "They went about their business, [and] they demonstrated respect for the other players."[2]

⊜ The Three-Peat

Despite the death of Joe DiMaggio on March 8, 1999, the Yankees' magic continued that season. On "Yogi Berra Day" on July 18, Don Larsen—who had tossed a perfect game in the 1956 World Series—threw out the ceremonial first pitch. Incredibly, that same afternoon, Yankees pitcher David Cone threw a perfect game of his own. New York won "only" 98 games in 1999, but their hitters were ferocious. Martinez, O'Neill, Jeter, and Williams all topped 100 RBIs, and Derek and Bernie hit over .340. Mariano Rivera posted 45 saves and a minuscule 1.83 ERA.

In the AL playoffs, New York swept Texas and beat the rival Red Sox in five games. After the Yankees took the first two World Series games in Atlanta, New York's Chad Curtis won Game 3 with a 10th-inning home run. The Yankees cruised 4–1 in Game 4 for their second straight World Series sweep. In the last major-league game of the

1900s, the New York Yankees—the team of the century—won their twenty-fifth world title.

Some of New York's stars continued to produce in 2000. Jeter ripped .339, Williams belted 30 homers, and switch-hitting catcher Jorge Posada knocked 28 out of the park. Yet too many players under-produced, most notably Martinez (.258) and Cone (4–14). Though 84–59 at one point, the Yankees lost sixteen of their last nineteen games and limped into the playoffs with just 87 total

▲ *Bernie Williams makes a spectacular one-handed grab. Williams was a vital part of the Yankees championship teams of the 1990s and early 2000s.*

wins. Yet, said manager Joe Torre, "I have a sense that what happened in the previous couple of weeks is not going to affect us."[3]

He was right. The proud, professional, and experienced Yankees romped again during the postseason. They defeated Oakland in the ALDS thanks to a six-run first inning in Game 5. In the ALCS against Seattle, Yankees pitcher Roger Clemens proved heroic. The gutsy fireballer— winner of five Cy Young Awards with Boston and Toronto—pitched the greatest game in League Championship Series history in Game 4: a one-hit, no-run, fifteen-strikeout masterpiece. New York prevailed in six games.

A day earlier, the New York Mets clinched the NLCS. Thus, all of New York was abuzz about the Big Apple World Series. *Newsweek* featured Jeter and Mets star Mike Piazza on the cover. "New York! New York!" blared the headline. "Hooray for the Subway Series."[4]

The Subway Series

The Yankees won the Series in five games, but every contest was special. The Yanks won Game 1 in the bottom of the 12th on an RBI single by light-hitting Jose Vizcaino. In Game 2, the Bronx Bombers won their fourteenth straight World Series game 6–5—although the Mets made it a thriller with 5 runs in the ninth. The Mets took the

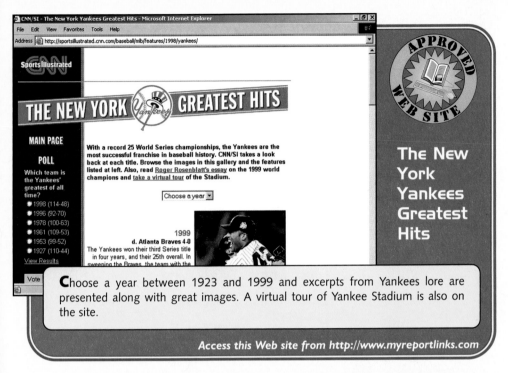

Choose a year between 1923 and 1999 and excerpts from Yankees lore are presented along with great images. A virtual tour of Yankee Stadium is also on the site.

Access this Web site from http://www.myreportlinks.com

next contest 4–2 with two runs in the eighth. Rivera saved a 3–2 win for the Bronx men in Game 4, and the Yankees won the finale 4–2 with two runs in the top of the ninth.

As champagne flowed in the Yankees' clubhouse, players chanted, "Three-peat! Three-peat! Three-peat!" The Yankees had become the first team since the 1972–74 Oakland A's to win three straight World Series.

Tragedy in New York

Never one to stand pat, Yankees owner George Steinbrenner signed another "stud" prior to the 2001 season: Baltimore Orioles pitcher Mike Mussina. Yet it was Roger "The Rocket" Clemens who propelled the Yankees to greatness. Clemens became the first pitcher in major-league history to start a season 20–1.

Clemens was scheduled to start on September 11, but tragedy interceded. Terrorist attacks on New York's World Trade Center killed nearly three thousand people. The Yankee players, like all Americans, were shocked and sickened. Second baseman Chuck Knoblauch watched the towers burn from his penthouse window. In the aftermath, Bernie Williams, Derek Jeter, and Paul O'Neill went to the Javits Center to comfort affected families that had gathered there.

Major-league games were canceled for a week. When play resumed, the Yankees honored New York firefighters and police officers who had lost their lives on 9/11 in a pregame ceremony. Branford Marsalis played "Taps," and the Harlem Boys Choir sang "We Shall Overcome."

The Playoffs

New York won the 2001 AL East title with 95 victories, but few were in a mood to celebrate. The Yankees' remarkable comeback in the ALDS—winning the last three games against Oakland after losing the first two—helped brighten the city's mournful mood. The Yanks demonstrated their character in the ALCS, defeating a Seattle team that had recorded an American League-record 116

Roger Clemens pitched for the Yankees from 1999 to 2003. In 2001, the Rocket went 20–3 and became the first pitcher to win six Cy Young Awards.

wins during the regular season.

In the World Series against Arizona, the Yankees rejuvenated New York with extraordinary comebacks in Games 4 and 5 (see Chapter 1). And though the Diamondbacks took Game 6 in a 15–2 rout, the Yankees seemed to have Game 7 under wraps. Not only did they lead 2–1 in the ninth inning, their all-star closer, Mariano Rivera, stood on the mound. The most successful postseason reliever ever, Rivera had saved 27 playoff/World Series games in 28 opportunities. But in his biggest game of all, he self-destructed.

Rivera allowed a single, flubbed a ball that was bunted to him, gave up a double, and hit a batter.

Then, with the bases loaded and the score 2–2, the Diamondbacks' Luis Gonzalez looped a broken-bat single to center to win the Series. Not since Bill Mazeroski's homer in 1960 had the Yankees swallowed such a bitter pill.

Big Bucks

By 2002, many of George Steinbrenner's fellow owners resented the Yankees boss. The Bronx Bombers' yearly revenue was enormous—well in excess of $200 million. Steinbrenner spent most of his money on player salaries. No other team team could compete with the Yanks' $140 million payroll. The Yankees, as well as the MLB Players' Association, did not want to put limits on how

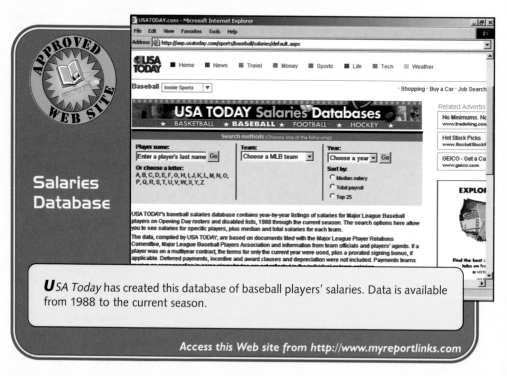

Salaries Database

USA Today has created this database of baseball players' salaries. Data is available from 1988 to the current season.

Access this Web site from http://www.myreportlinks.com

much New York and other wealthy teams could spend. The dispute nearly led to a players strike in August 2002. Only at the last minute did negotiators avert a work stoppage.

Jason Giambi was the new poster boy for Yankees money. In December 2001, New York signed the former Oakland A's slugger to a seven-year, $120-million contract. And he delivered. Giambi belted 41 homers in 2002, sparking the Yanks to 103 victories. However, the Anaheim Angels were the team of destiny that fall, beating New York in four ALDS games en route to the world title.

The Curse

The Yankees' dominance over the Red Sox had existed since 1920, when Boston sold Babe Ruth to New York. For Sox fans in 2003, the "curse" became pure torment. The Yankees and Red Sox were playoff bound that year, and they battled each other intensely throughout the season. Sox fans uttered unkind words when the Yankees visited Fenway Park. New Yorkers responded by chanting "1918! 1918!"—the year Boston last won a World Series—when the Red Sox were in town. The Yankees won the AL East title with 101 victories, while Boston made the playoffs as a wildcard. Fatefully, they wound up facing each other in the ALCS.

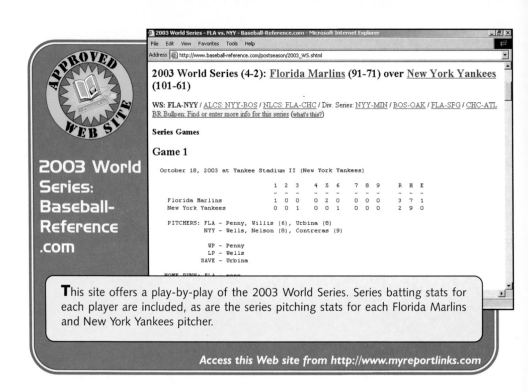

2003 World Series - FLA vs. NYY - Baseball-Reference.com - Microsoft Internet Explorer

File   Edit   View   Favorites   Tools   Help

Address   http://www.baseball-reference.com/postseason/2003_WS.shtml

2003 World Series (4-2): Florida Marlins (91-71) over New York Yankees (101-61)

WS: FLA-NYY / ALCS: NYY-BOS / NLCS: FLA-CHC / Div. Series: NYY-MIN / BOS-OAK / FLA-SFG / CHC-ATL
BR Bullpen: Find or enter more info for this series (what's this?)

Series Games

Game 1

October 18, 2003 at Yankee Stadium II (New York Yankees)

```
                      1 2 3   4 5 6   7 8 9    R H E
                      - - -   - - -   - - -    - - -
    Florida Marlins   1 0 0   0 2 0   0 0 0    3 7 1
    New York Yankees  0 0 1   0 0 1   0 0 0    2 9 0

    PITCHERS: FLA - Penny, Willis (6), Urbina (8)
              NYY - Wells, Nelson (8), Contreras (9)

              WP - Penny
              LP - Wells
              SAVE - Urbina

    HOME RUNS: FLA - none
```

This site offers a play-by-play of the 2003 World Series. Series batting stats for each player are included, as are the series pitching stats for each Florida Marlins and New York Yankees pitcher.

Access this Web site from http://www.myreportlinks.com

In Game 3 at Fenway, tensions reached full boil. Each team accused the other team's pitcher of throwing at hitters. When New York's Roger Clemens fired a pitch near Manny Ramirez's head, players from both dugouts charged onto the field. During the melee, Boston pitcher Pedro Martinez slammed seventy-two-year-old Yankees coach Don Zimmer to the ground. Players later apologized, but the bad blood continued.

Prior to Game 7, Clemens patted Babe Ruth's monument at Yankee Stadium for good luck. The Red Sox held a 5–2 lead in the eighth inning, yet New York rallied for three runs in the bottom of the eighth to tie. Then, leading off the bottom of the 11th, Yankees third baseman Aaron Boone rocketed a shot into the left-field seats. Boone leaped into his teammates' arms at home plate, while Red Sox players fell to their knees in heart-break. The curse, it seemed, would plague them forever.

Perhaps drained by the emotional Red Sox series, the Yankees were upset by the Florida Marlins in the 2003 World Series, losing in six games. Shortstop Alex Gonzalez delivered the killer blow, belting a walk-off homer in the 12th inning of Game 4. George Steinbrenner responded to the defeat the only way he knew how: Spend more money.

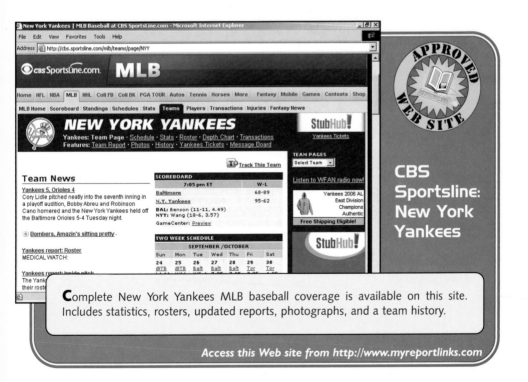

CBS Sportsline: New York Yankees

Complete New York Yankees MLB baseball coverage is available on this site. Includes statistics, rosters, updated reports, photographs, and a team history.

Access this Web site from http://www.myreportlinks.com

⊜The A-Rod Era

On February 16, 2004, the Yankees traded all-star second baseman Alfonso Soriano to the Texas Rangers for Alex Rodriguez. Steinbrenner acquired not just the greatest power-hitting short-stop of all time, but the largest contract as well. A-Rod was in the midst of a ten-year, $252-million deal. Because Derek Jeter was already firmly entrenched at shortstop, A-Rod made the switch to third base without complaint.

Rodgriguez clubbed 36 homers in a subpar year in 2004. Superstar Gary Sheffield, another new acquisition, also knocked 36 longballs. Together, they led the Yankees to 101 wins and

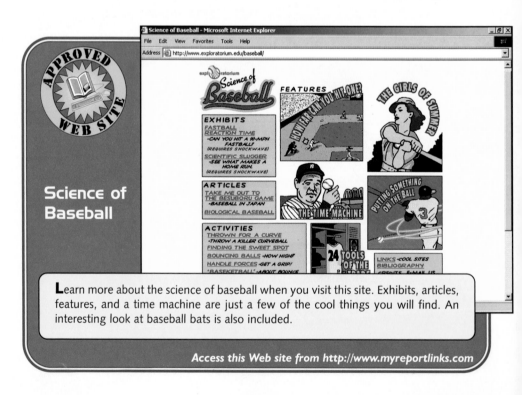

Science of Baseball

Learn more about the science of baseball when you visit this site. Exhibits, articles, features, and a time machine are just a few of the cool things you will find. An interesting look at baseball bats is also included.

Access this Web site from http://www.myreportlinks.com

the division title. With New York and Boston both prevailing in the ALDS, Red Sox fans braced themselves for a sequel to 2003's ALCS horror show.

Boston Busts the Curse

At first, that is how the 2004 ALCS played out. The Yankees won the first two games in the Bronx, 10–7 and 3–1, before massacring the Beantowners 19–8 at Fenway. At that point, Red Sox Nation called it a season. They knew the reality: No team in major-league history—dating back to the 1903 World Series—had ever rallied from an 0–3 deficit to win a postseason series.

Then again, the Red Sox were "a team that never gives up," said Boston slugger David Ortiz.[5] Down 3–2 in the bottom of the ninth of Game 4, and facing preeminent closer Mariano Rivera, the Red Sox rallied to tie. In the 12th inning, at 1:22 A.M., Ortiz belted a walk-off home run. Incredibly, Ortiz delivered another dramatic hit the next night, singling home the game-winning run in the 14th.

The Red Sox still had to win Games 6 and 7, both in New York, but this time the Yankees felt the tug of the choke collar. Boston won each game, 4–2 and 10–3. Red Sox owner John Henry rightfully called it "the greatest comeback in baseball history."[6] From their living rooms, the Yankees watched an elated Red Sox team soar past the

▲ Starting pitcher Chien-Ming Wang went 19–6 for the Yankees during the 2006 season. That set a record for the most wins in a season by an Asian-born player.

St. Louis Cardinals in four games in the World Series. Even the staunchest Yankees fans had to admit the truth: The "Curse of the Bambino" was over.

In 2005, the Yankees added five-time Cy Young Award winner Randy Johnson to the mix. With big-name pitchers and eight current or former all-stars in the lineup, the Yankees packed the stadium every game. For the first time in team history, they drew more than 4 million fans. Rodriguez, the biggest star of all, smashed 48 home runs to win the AL MVP Award.

The Yankees struggled all year to make the playoffs, and did so only on the last weekend. Manager Joe Torre won his ninth division title with the Bombers and took his team to the post-season for the tenth time in ten tries. But alas, the Yankees lost in the ALDS, three games to two to the Los Angeles Angels of Anaheim.

When Giambi and Sheffield were sidelined with injuries in 2006, the Yankees acquired star out-fielder Bobby Abreu in midseason. He helped the Bombers win an AL-best 97 games. When Jason and Gary returned late in the season, New York boasted a lineup of nine current or former all-stars. The Yankees were expected to cruise past Detroit in the ALDS, but their supposedly explosive bats fell limp. New York lost in four games, concluding their fifth straight year of bitter disappointment.

Miller Huggins won 2,569 games over a seventeen-year career while managing the St. Louis Cardinals and New York Yankees. He was elected to the National Baseball Hall of Fame in 1964.

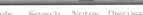

THE MASTERMINDS

5

Throughout their storied history, the Yankees owners have been willing to spend big bucks for championship-level players. They have also hired the right people to acquire, develop, and manage that talent. Featured below are the masterminds behind the Yankees' 26 world titles, as well as a pair of broadcasters who kept fan interest alive for more than a half century.

Miller Huggins

In 1919, the Yankees failed again to win a pennant. Manager Miller Huggins knew what the team needed. "Get [Babe] Ruth from Boston," he reportedly told team owner Jacob Ruppert. "Bring him to the Polo Grounds and he'll hit 35 homers at least."[1]

Huggins's hunch was dead-on, and the deal for Ruth went through. Yet over the next decade, the

65

relationship between Ruth and his manager was almost comically bad. In contrast to the Babe, Huggins was a tiny, cerebral man who believed in strict personal discipline. The partying slugger and the skipper known as "Mighty Mite" bickered almost constantly. In July 1925, Ruth actually dangled his manager out a train window. A month later, Huggins fined and suspended the Babe. Ruppert sided with Huggins, and from then on Ruth knew not to cross his manager.

In the 1920s, Huggins led talented Yankees clubs to six American League pennants and three World Series titles. Remembered pitcher Waite Hoyt, "Huggins was almost like a schoolmaster in the dugout. There was no goofing off. You watched the game, and you kept track not only of the score and the number of outs, but of the count on the batter."[2]

While active as the Yankees manager in 1929, Huggins died of a skin disease at age fifty. Ruth, who had grown to appreciate his longtime manager, broke into tears when he heard the news.

Ed Barrow

Boston's disdain for the Yankees dates back to 1920, and not just because the Red Sox sold Babe Ruth to the Yanks that year. Shortly after the 1920 season, Boston manager Ed Barrow signed with the Yankees as their general manager.

Subsequently, he tormented the Red Sox with one lopsided trade after another.

The stern man with the bushy eyebrows was one of the shrewdest guys in baseball. He had managed the Red Sox to the world title in 1918, and he had served as president of two minor leagues. Just six weeks after becoming Yankees GM, he acquired a future Hall of Fame pitcher (Waite Hoyt) and a .300-hitting catcher (Wally Schang) from Boston while giving the Red Sox little in return.

The Yankees owners had a generous budget, and Barrow spent the money wisely. In addition to his wily trades, he occasionally acquired veteran stars for cash. He also signed such future legends

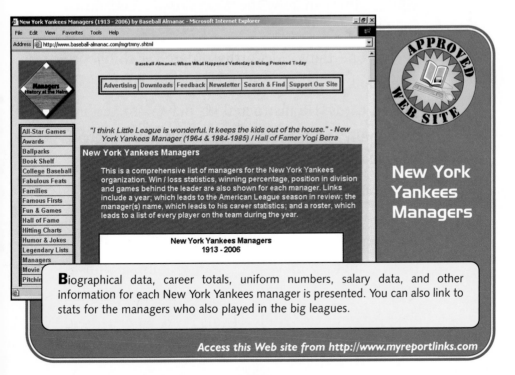

New York Yankees Managers

Biographical data, career totals, uniform numbers, salary data, and other information for each New York Yankees manager is presented. You can also link to stats for the managers who also played in the big leagues.

Access this Web site from http://www.myreportlinks.com

as Lou Gehrig and Joe DiMaggio, and he helped develop a prolific farm system. The Yankees not only made the World Series fourteen times during Barrow's twenty-five years with the team, but they also won ten fall classics—half of which were sweeps. A plaque at Yankee Stadium honors Barrow, calling him a "moulder of a tradition of victory."

Joe McCarthy

The 1930 Yankees overflowed with talent, but the club finished a disappointing third in the American League. Joe McCarthy, hired as manager for the next season, believed the team lacked discipline. Immediately, the new skipper laid down the law.

For one thing, McCarthy ordered a clubhouse attendant to destroy the table where the Yankees played cards. He instructed his players to act professionally and focus completely on baseball. During road trips, all players had to show up for breakfast at 8:30—in a jacket and tie.

Reporters poked fun at McCarthy for his dull personality and for using the same lineup almost every single game. They called him a "push-button manager." However, the skipper juggled his pitchers masterfully. He also was an alert field general and a marvelous teacher. Said Joe

DiMaggio, "Never a day went by when you didn't learn something from McCarthy."[3]

As a result, McCarthy maximized the talents of his players. From 1931 to 1946, he led New York to six 100-win seasons and seven world titles—including four in a row beginning in 1936. His career winning percentage of .615 remains the best in major-league history.

⊜ Mel Allen

Most Yankees fans did not own a television set in the 1940s. But they had the next best thing: broadcaster Mel Allen on the radio. With his easy southern drawl and sunny disposition, the "Voice of the Yankees" made every game a delight.

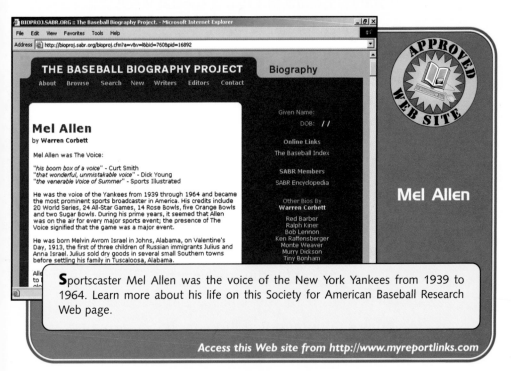

Sportscaster Mel Allen was the voice of the New York Yankees from 1939 to 1964. Learn more about his life on this Society for American Baseball Research Web page.

Access this Web site from http://www.myreportlinks.com

Allen joined the team's broadcast booth in 1940, booming enthusiasm across New York. He gave Joe DiMaggio and Phil Rizzuto their famous nicknames—the "Yankee Clipper" and "The Scooter." In 1948, he introduced his trademark home run call. As an outfielder drifted back to the fence, he intoned, "It's going, going . . . gone!" When a Yankees play was just too exciting for words, he exclaimed, "How about that!"

Allen also broadcast All-Star Games and World Series games for NBC-TV. He recalled: "One year, *Variety* ran a list of the most recognizable voices in the world . . . Churchill, Roosevelt, people like that. I was the only sports announcer on the list. I guess then I realized I had a special voice."[4]

Allen toiled for the Yankees until 1964. He then made a comeback in 1977 as the host of the hugely popular television show *This Week in Baseball.* In 1978, he and Red Barber were the first broadcasters enshrined in the Baseball Hall of Fame.

Phil Rizzuto

"Uh-oh," uttered Yankees broadcaster Phil Rizzuto. "Deep to left-center. Nobody's gonna get that one! Holy cow, somebody got it!"

Rizzuto was not the slickest broadcaster in baseball. But with his charm, enthusiasm, and sometimes unintentional humor, he entertained fans on radio and television for forty years.

▲ Phil Rizzuto announces his retirement from broadcasting on August 23, 1995. After a public outcry from his fans, he returned to the booth on a part-time basis in 1996.

"The Scooter" joined the Yankees in 1941 and contributed to their five straight world championships after the war. He dazzled defensively at shortstop, and when he cracked .324 in 1950, he won the American League MVP Award. Upon his retirement in 1956, he joined the Yankees broadcast booth.

Rizzuto displayed as much excitement at the microphone as he had on the field. Besides his trademark "Holy cow!" he often exclaimed "Unbelievable!" and "Did you see that?" He also championed the use of the bunt, at which he was a master during his playing days. Moreover, Rizzuto connected intimately with those who tuned in. He often sent out get-well or happy birthday wishes to fans across New York.

Over the years, Rizzuto teamed with such broadcast legends as Red Barber, Mel Allen, and Joe Garagiola. The Yankees retired his uniform No. 10 in 1985, and he himself retired in 1996— fifty-five years after his rookie season.

⊜ Casey Stengel

Frustrated by his performance one day, Mickey Mantle smashed the dugout's water supply. Manager Casey Stengel looked at his young slugger and snapped: "Son, it ain't the water cooler that's striking you out."[5]

▲ Manager Casey Stengel poses with star player Mickey Mantle in this 1957 photo. Stengel was perhaps the most well-liked manager in baseball history.

The response was pure Stengel. It reflected his butchered English, his sense of humor, and his ability to use sarcasm to light a fire under his troops. One of the great characters in baseball history, Stengel also ranked among the most savvy and successful managers ever.

A big-league outfielder from 1912 to 1925, Stengel learned the game from legendary New York Giants manager John McGraw. After managing the Brooklyn Dodgers and Boston Braves, Casey took over as Yankees skipper in 1949. Incredibly, he won world championships in his first five seasons at the helm.

The Platoon

Stengel became famous for platooning his players—using left-handed batters against right-handed pitchers and vice versa. Moreover, his instincts for the game were uncanny. "He made what some people call stupid moves," recalled pitcher Don Larsen, "but about eight or nine out of ten of them worked."[6]

In twelve years with the Yankees, "The Old Perfessor" won ten American League pennants and seven world titles. He later managed the woeful New York Mets, retiring at age seventy-five in 1965. Looking back on his fifty-five years in the game, he remarked, "There comes a time in every man's life and I've had plenty of 'em."[7]

→ George Steinbrenner

When George Steinbrenner bought the Yankees for $10 million in 1973, he insisted he would be a "hands-off" owner. "My other interests—shipbuilding, horseracing, etc.—keep me busy," he said. "I'd be silly trying to run a ballclub, too."[8]

Yet it was not long before Steinbrenner became the most active owner baseball fans had ever seen. He delved heavily into free agency, signing such stars as Catfish Hunter and Reggie Jackson to record-breaking contracts. "The Boss" expected world championships, and when the

ESPN Classic - 'The Boss' made Yankees a dictatorship - Microsoft Internet Explorer

Address http://espn.go.com/classic/biography/s/Steinbrenner_George.html

ESPN Network: ESPN.com | NBA.com | NHL.com | WNBA.com | ABCSports | EXPN | INSIDER | FANTASY

SPORTSCENTURY | CLASSIC MOMENTS | SCHEDULE

Sports Sections
MLB
NBA
NFL
NHL
College Football
Men's Basketball
Golf
Motorsports
Women's Hoops
Tennis
Boxing
College Sports
Olympic Sports
U.S. Soccer
Horses
Poker
Outdoors | BASS
ProRodeo | WNFR

SPORTSCENTURY BIOGRAPHY

'The Boss' made Yankees a dictatorship

By Mike Puma
Special to ESPN.com

"If things go right, they're his team. If things go wrong, they're your team. His favorite line is, 'I will never have a heart attack. I give them,'" **says former Yankees general manager Bob Watson about George Steinbrenner on ESPN Classic's SportsCentury series.**

He equates owning the New York Yankees to possessing the Mona Lisa. Both are masterpieces to be savored, not sold. Since purchasing the franchise in 1973, George Steinbrenner has run the Yankees with a flair that has made him -- loved or hated -- the most prominent owner in sports.

Steinbrenner has a bombastic, calculating and cold side that transformed the Yankees into baseball's foremost dictatorship. The other side of Steinbrenner is the philanthropist and father figure

George Steinbrenner, who bought the Yankees in 1973, is the most prominent owner in sports.

Shipbuilding tycoon George Steinbrenner bought the Yankees in 1973. In this online article, **"'The Boss' Made Yankees a Dictatorship,"** you can learn about the team under his reign.

EDITOR'S CHOICE

team did not deliver, he often blamed the manager. In his first seventeen seasons as Yankees owner, he changed managers seventeen times. To his credit, New York did win the World Series in 1977 and 1978.

After a long drought without a championship, Steinbrenner built a winner again in the mid-1990s. He had mellowed by this time, and he let his general manager and manager make the day-to-day decisions. Yes, he continued to sign players to huge contracts. But his wisest decision was to retain Joe Torre as his manager for more than a decade. The result: four world titles from 1996 to 2000.

Billy Martin

When *The Bronx Zoo* was published in 1979, the book had nothing to do with the home for animals on New York's Southern Boulevard. The "zoo" referred to the Yankees, and Billy Martin was its "keeper."

As a Yankees second baseman in the 1950s, Martin was tough and scrappy. He won the World Series MVP Award in 1953, but New York traded him in 1957 after he instigated a nightclub brawl. He later became famous as an ingenious but volatile manager. From the 1960s to the 1980s, he turned Minnesota, Detroit, Texas, and Oakland into contenders. Yet due to his temper, he never lasted more than three years with any of those ballclubs.

When Yankees owner George Steinbrenner hired Martin in 1975, the new manager immediately lit a spark under the team. Recalled outfielder Roy White: "Billy let us do so many things . . . hit and run, pull running bunt plays, double-steal. It drove the opposition nuts."[9] Martin led New York to the world title in 1977. However, he frequently butted heads with Steinbrenner as well as his players, especially superstar Reggie Jackson.

Steinbrenner fired Martin in July 1978, but the manager's relationship with the team was far from over. Over the next decade, the Yankees owner hired and fired Martin as manager four more times. "Billy the Kid" died in a car crash on Christmas Day, 1989.

Joe Torre

When Joe Torre was hired to manage the Yankees in November 1995, some New Yorkers were skeptical. Torre had played or managed in the National League for thirty-one years and had never won the World Series. Moreover, his dour expression turned people off. Was this really the best man to end the Yankees' seventeen-year championship drought?

You bet. First off, Torre brought NL-style baseball to the American League. He had his players

▲ This dugout photo was taken during spring training in 1988. From left to right are then Manager Billy Martin, owner George Steinbrenner, and then General Manager Lou Piniella.

bunt, steal, hit-and-run, and generally keep their opponents on edge. His even-keel personality reassured his troops. Off the field, he demanded that his players maintain a high level of professionalism.

Yes, Torre had the best talent that owner George Steinbrenner could buy. But he maximized that talent, leading the Yankees to six AL pennants and four world titles from 1996 through 2003. With a league-record 114 wins in 1998, Torre was named AL Manager of the Year.

Yankee legends are honored in Monument Park, behind the center-field fence in Yankee Stadium. This photo was taken in 1999 when Joe DiMaggio's monument was unveiled.

WELCOME TO YANKEE STADIUM

6

A Yankees fan from New Jersey remembered one of his first trips to Yankee Stadium. Like most out-of-towners, he was a bit apprehensive about the visit. New York, after all, is an overwhelming city of 8 million people. The South Bronx, where the ballpark stands, is a poor, crime-ridden area. Outside the stadium, the New Jerseyan became unnerved when a local man walked straight toward him. But the oncoming stranger quickly reassured him with a friendly gesture. "Yankee baseball," said the local man with a smile. "There is nothing in the *world* better, is there?"[1] The two Yankee fans then greeted each other with high fives.

The House That Ruth Built

Babe Ruth did not literally build Yankee Stadium, but he did generate the revenue to finance the construction. In fact, in the early 1920s, the Yankees considered building a one hundred thousand-seat ballpark to accommodate all of Ruth's fans. The original Yankee Stadium, completed in 1923, seated eighty thousand patrons. The project was a grand undertaking, costing $2.5 million. It featured not two but three decks, shaped like a horseshoe. Bleachers and a scoreboard were constructed in the outfield. On the stadium's exterior, a distinctive copper facade circled the top of the ballpark.

Originally, the center-field fence stood 490 feet away from home plate. It was so far that in 1932 the Yankees built a monument to late manager Miller Huggins in deep center—in play. In the 1940s, monuments honoring Babe Ruth and Lou Gehrig were built next to Huggins's monument. Once, when a Yankee opponent blasted a drive to deep center field, manager Casey Stengel yelled, "Ruth! Gehrig! Huggins! Somebody throw that thing in here!"[2]

A Welcomed Renovation

In 1974 and 1975, the Yankees remodeled their ballpark. Workers replaced the copper facade with a replica. They lowered the upper decks and tilted them on a steeper angle so fans could see better. They replaced the old wooden seats with wider, plastic ones. They also installed a state-of-the-art "telescreen." The renovated park accommodated only fifty-four thousand fans, but nearly every seat was a good one.

Yankee Stadium's outfield dimensions favor left-handed hitters who pull the ball. The distances to the fence are 314 feet down the right-field line, 385 in right-center, and 408 in center field. Left-center is nicknamed "Death Valley" (399 feet), while the left-field foul pole rests 318 feet from home plate. In the 1940s and the 1950s, fans wondered how many homers right-hander Joe DiMaggio would have hit if his fly balls had not died in Death Valley.

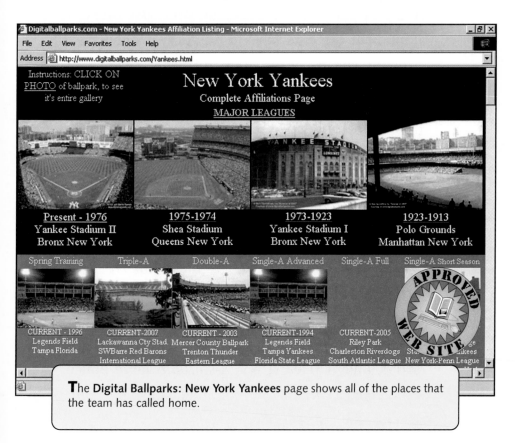

The **Digital Ballparks: New York Yankees** page shows all of the places that the team has called home.

The Yankee monuments still stand, including one honoring Mickey Mantle, but they are now located behind the center-field fence. Visitors are welcomed to visit "Monument Park," which also features plaques of other Yankee legends as well as all of the team's retired uniform numbers. The team has retired sixteen numbers, including 1, 3, 4, 5, 7, 8, and 9. Since Derek Jeter's No. 2 and Joe Torre's No. 6 will likely be retired someday, that would not leave any single-digit numbers.

Game Day

You will never forget attending your first Yankees game, but first you have to buy tickets—and they are not cheap. As of 2006, bleacher seats sold for $12 and Tier Reserved—way up in the third deck—were $19 to $20. The best seats in the house are called Field Championship ($98–115), Loge Championship ($98–100), and Main Championship ($80–85). All other tickets range from $40 to $75.

While Yankee Stadium provides parking, most patrons take the subway to the ballpark. Fans arrive to a festive, noisy scene. Amid the rumble of the nearby trains, thousands of fans chatter outside the park. Outdoor vendors sell hot dogs, sodas, and "I [Heart] NY" T-shirts. A large police force makes sure Mr. Steinbrenner's fans feel comfortably safe.

If you get to the park early, you can stroll down River Avenue, which is lined with restaurants and souvenir shops. Serious fans like to hang out at Stan's Sports Bar and Restaurant. The famous Court Deli is two blocks east of the stadium on 161st Street and Walton. It is worth the walk if you crave a thick, lean corned beef sandwich.

Once inside Yankee Stadium, you will immediately sense the history of the grand, old ballpark. Right field is not just well-manicured lawn; it is where Babe Ruth once roamed. Lou Gehrig kicked the dirt around first base, and Don Larsen pitched

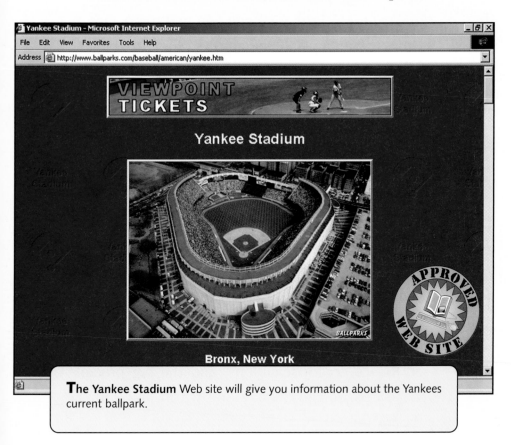

The Yankee Stadium Web site will give you information about the Yankees current ballpark.

a perfect game on the pitcher's mound. Your game experience will depend on where you sit. The bleachers attract many working-class New Yorkers. No beer is permitted in this area due to a history of rowdy behavior by bleacher fans. Those who sit in the third deck need binoculars and a strong constitution: The high altitude and steep angle of the seats is a bit scary.

Many fans wear Yankees caps and jackets at the game. They tend to be highly knowledgeable about baseball and—as New Yorkers—love to chat. Thus, you might end up talking baseball for two hours with a person you had never met. If you want to buy Yankees clothes of your own, you better start saving. Official caps sell for up to $25, while jackets range from $60 to $450.

The Game Experience

Being that New York is an expensive place to live, concession prices are a little higher than at most big-league parks. Yet on hot summer days, fans will gladly pay $4.75 for fresh-squeezed lemonade. Most of the ballpark food is standard, but vendors also sell sushi and a wide variety of hot dogs and sausages—including a Hebrew National kosher wiener. Kids are pleased to see a wide variety of ice cream selections, and the big pretzels are crispy on the outside and warm and soft on the inside.

Since the Yankees are title contenders year after year, the stadium is usually packed to capacity. By game time, public address announcer Bob Sheppard takes to the mike. Born in 1910, Sheppard in 2005 celebrated his fifty-fifth year as the Yankees' PA man. With his deep, booming voice that seems to emanate from the heavens, Sheppard sounds like the "voice of God," according to Reggie Jackson.[3] Sheppard introduces every new batter the same way: "Now batting for the Yankees, the center fielder, Bernie Williams . . . No. 51."

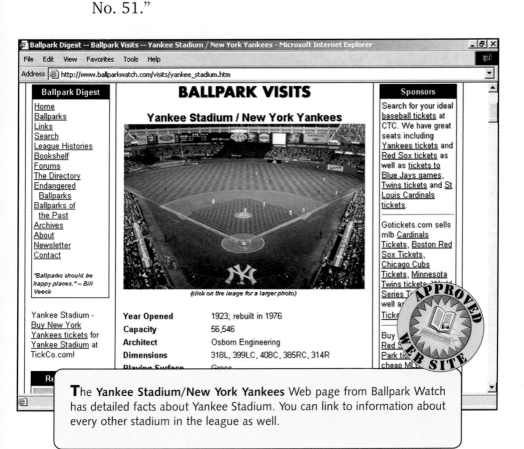

The **Yankee Stadium/New York Yankees** Web page from Ballpark Watch has detailed facts about Yankee Stadium. You can link to information about every other stadium in the league as well.

During the "Seventh-Inning Stretch," everyone stands for Kate Smith's recording of "God Bless America," followed by an organ rendition of "Take Me Out to the Ballgame." On a good day at the stadium, Alex Rodriguez will crack a home run, Derek Jeter will spark a big rally, and closing pitcher Mariano Rivera will save the game. When the Yankees win, Frank Sinatra's "New York, New York" is played and all Yankees fans go home happy.

Big Business

In 1973, Yankees owner George Steinbrenner made one of the greatest investments in America. He and his partners bought the Yankees for $10 million. And although he now says the team is invaluable—"Owning the Yankees is like owning the Mona Lisa," he says—outsiders value the club at approximately $1 billion.[4] It is the most valuable franchise in the history of sports.

Though a baseball team, the Yankees are very much a business. The front office boasts seventeen executives with the rank of vice president or higher. Departments include stadium operations, finance, tickets, marketing, sales, community relations, concessions, scouting, and so on. On game day, part-time employees swarm to the ballpark. They work as food vendors, groundskeepers, ushers, security guards, etc. During each game, the Yankees employ approximately two thousand workers. Moreover, the Yankees operate a baseball farm (minor-league) system. Their minor-league teams include Scranton-Wilkes Barre (AAA), Trenton (AA), and four lower-level clubs. From 1979 to 2006, the Yankees AAA club was the Columbus Clippers. Scranton-Wilkes Barre began play as a Yankees affiliate in 2007.

The Yankees make, and spend, more money than any other baseball club. In 2005, the team generated approximately $335 million. A large chunk of that income came from ticket revenue, while the YES cable company contributed about

The first place to go for up-to-date news about the Bronx Bombers is the **New York Yankees Official Site** brought to you by Major League Baseball.

EDITOR'S CHOICE

$60 million for the rights to broadcast Yankee games. The team also made tens of millions of dollars from concession and merchandise sales.

No Easy Money

Despite this influx of money, the Yankees spent more than they made in 2005. They paid their players an astronomical $213 million. Alex Rodriguez topped the list at $26 million, while Derek Jeter earned $19.6 million and Mike Mussina $19 million.

In addition, the Yankees had to pay a $34 million "luxury tax." According to the rules of Major League Baseball, if a team's payroll exceeded $128 million, it was taxed on the excess. This taxed money was distributed to "small-market" teams that did not generate much income, such as the Kansas City Royals and Minnesota Twins. This is called "revenue sharing," and it is meant to help "poorer" teams be competitive.

According to the *New York Daily News,* the Yankees lost $50 million to $85 million in 2005.[5] Had the team made the World Series, it would have come much closer to breaking even. After the season, the Yankees announced they would trim their player payroll. Yet in December, the team signed All-Star center fielder Johnny Damon to a four-year, $52 million contract. Steinbrenner, with his passion for winning, just could not resist.

⊘ Following the Yankees

"Yankees win!" blares radio broadcaster John Sterling about one hundred times a year. "Thaaaaaaa Yankees win!" With his resonant, melodic voice, Sterling has brought Yankees games to life on WCBS (880 AM) since 1989. In 2005, he welcomed a new partner to the booth. Award-winning journalist Suzyn Waldman took over as the Yankees' color commentator. She thus became the first woman to hold a full-time position as a major-league broadcaster.

Yankees fans in the New York area follow the team on the YES (Yankees Entertainment & Sports) Network. YES broadcasts approximately

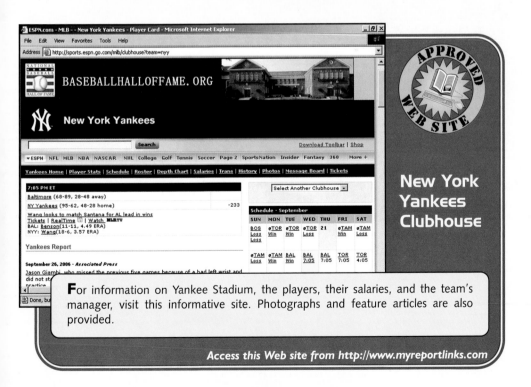

New York Yankees Clubhouse

For information on Yankee Stadium, the players, their salaries, and the team's manager, visit this informative site. Photographs and feature articles are also provided.

Access this Web site from http://www.myreportlinks.com

New York Governor George Pataki speaks to the crowd on August 16, 2006. This press conference was held to announce the start of construction on a new Yankee Stadium. An image of what the new stadium will look like is in the background.

130 games a year. The highly professional Michael Kay does the play-by-play, while former major-league all-stars Jim Kaat, Bobby Murcer, and Ken Singleton serve as analysts. For fans who cannot get enough, YES offers such shows as *Yankees Classics, Yankeeography,* and *Yankees Hot Stove.*

Over the last decade, the Yankees have been on national television more than any other American sports team—mostly on FOX and ESPN. Fans around the world can keep up with the team on its official Web site. The site even includes an impressive kids section. For a fee, youngsters can join the Yankees Fan Club. Members receive a Yankees T-shirt, discounts on tickets, and more than a dozen other Yankees goodies.

The New Yankee Stadium

In June 2005, the Yankees announced plans for a new Yankee Stadium. Baseball fans nearly fell out of their seats when they heard how much it would cost: $1 billion!

The new ballpark will be located just north of the current stadium and will seat 51,800 fans. To maintain team tradition, the park will look remarkably similar to the "House That Ruth Built." The field dimensions will remain the same, as will the bullpen area. In fact, the new structure will include some of the features of the old stadium before it was renovated in the 1970s. For example, the exterior of the new stadium will be unpainted limestone and concrete.

The Yankees themselves will finance approximately $800 million of the project. George Steinbrenner believes that higher-priced tickets, expensive luxury suites, and more concession stands will generate greater revenue. However, many New Yorkers feel that the new project is a waste of money. Said David Gratt, president of Friends of Yankee Stadium, "The current stadium should be renovated rather than torn down. The city shouldn't be spending money on it. It isn't a public good, it's a private one."[6]

New York Governor George Pataki disagrees:

> This is an exciting public-private plan for Yankee Stadium that will truly transform the South Bronx. Not only will New York get a new Yankee Stadium but our city will get over 3,600 construction jobs, a new waterfront park, as well as many other traffic, streetscape, and infrastructure improvements. This is a smart investment in the future of the Bronx that will yield hundreds of millions of dollars in revenue in the coming years.[7]

A large number of New York journalists embraced the undertaking. Wrote T. J. Quinn of the *New York Daily News,* "Even the Babe would be proud."[8] The Yankees hope to open the new ballpark in 2009.

Babe Ruth embraces former Yankees teammate Lou Gehrig on July 14, 1939. Gehrig gave an emotional speech, thanking the fans for their support as he battled his fatal illness.

THE HEROES

If assembling a baseball "dream team," one could load the lineup with New York Yankees. Babe Ruth and Lou Gehrig would start in right field and first base, and perhaps Joe DiMaggio, Mickey Mantle, Yogi Berra, and/or Alex Rodriguez would earn starting nods. In their storied history, the Yankees have fielded forty-one Hall of Famers and more superstars than any other major-league franchise.

➲ Babe Ruth

For decades, baseball was a game of singles, doubles, bunts, and steals. Then along came Babe Ruth. "I swing big, with everything I've got," Ruth said. "I hit big or I miss big. I like to live as big as I can."[1]

As a lefty pitcher with the Boston Red Sox, Ruth averaged 20 wins a year from 1915 through

1918. As a hitter, he slugged a major-league record 29 homers in 1919 before revolutionizing the sport as a Yankee. The Babe not only demolished his longball record with 54 round-trippers in 1920, but he also out-homered every other AL team that year. Forevermore, the nation became infatuated with home runs.

In 1921, Ruth socked 59 home runs, drove in 171, and scored 177. In 1927, he walloped 60 four-baggers—a big-league record that would stand for thirty-four years. When his salary exceeded President Herbert Hoover's earnings in 1930, Ruth replied—correctly—"Why not? I had a better year than he did."[2]

Ruth led the American League in home runs in twelve different seasons. At the time of his death in 1948, he owned fifty-six major-league records. Included were career records for home runs (714), RBI (2,217), slugging average (.690), walks (2,062), and on-base percentage (.474). He also posted a career batting average of .342.

Due to his prowess as a slugger and pitcher, Ruth has been rated as the greatest baseball player ever in virtually every poll of experts. In 2000, the Associated Press rated the Babe as the greatest athlete of the twentieth century.

Lou Gehrig

All three of Lou Gehrig's siblings died before reaching adulthood. Gehrig, though, seemed as if

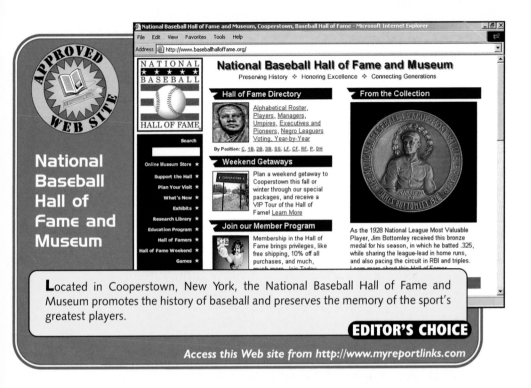

National Baseball Hall of Fame and Museum

Located in Cooperstown, New York, the National Baseball Hall of Fame and Museum promotes the history of baseball and preserves the memory of the sport's greatest players.

EDITOR'S CHOICE

Access this Web site from http://www.myreportlinks.com

he were indestructible. A quiet man of great character, he played in 2,130 consecutive games as the Yankees' first baseman. Not even fractured bones in his hand sidelined the "Iron Horse."

Unquestionably, Gehrig rates as the greatest hitting infielder of all time. Batting cleanup behind Babe Ruth, he bashed .373 with 47 homers and 175 RBIs in 1927. Three years later, he cracked .379 and drove in 174. In his thirteen full seasons, Gehrig averaged a staggering 147 RBIs per year. His 23 grand slams (out of 493 career homers) remain a major-league record.

In 1939, however, tragedy struck the fourth Gehrig child. Feeling progressively weak, Gehrig checked himself into the Mayo Clinic. Doctors diagnosed him with amyotrophic lateral sclerosis. "Lou Gehrig's Disease," as it became known, was incurable. On June 3, 1941, New Yorkers wept when they heard the news: Lou Gehrig, just thirty-seven years old, had passed away.

Joe DiMaggio

Every game, every play, Joe DiMaggio gave it all he had. "There is always some kid who may be seeing me for the first or last time," he explained. "I owe him my best."[3]

For thirteen seasons with the Yankees, "Joltin' Joe" patrolled center field with grace and class. His 56-game hitting streak in 1941 captivated the nation. Yet the achievement was just a small portion of his epic career.

The son of a fisherman, DiMaggio first made his mark with the minor-league San Francisco Seals, hitting in 61 consecutive games in 1933. As a twenty-two-year-old Yankee in 1937, he posted staggering statistics: a .346 batting average, 46 home runs, and 167 RBIs. Two years later, he bashed .381 and won his first of three AL MVP Awards.

An all-star every season, DiMaggio led the Yankees to ten World Series, winning nine of them. He played a flawless center field, and ran the bases like a gazelle. He rarely struck out. And,

The Official Site of Joe DiMaggio honors the memory of the Yankee Clipper. DiMaggio led the Yankees to nine World Series championships.

said Yankees manager Joe McCarthy, he "never made a mental mistake."[4] In 1969, Major League Baseball named DiMaggio the game's "Greatest Living Player."

Yogi Berra

Yankees catcher Yogi Berra once met Mary Lindsay, wife of New York Mayor John Lindsay. She told him that he looked nice and cool in his summer suit. "Thanks," he replied. "You don't look so hot yourself."[5]

Throughout his career (and beyond), Berra became famous for his humorous, confusing quotes. "It ain't over till it's over" and "It's getting late early" are among the "Yogi-isms" that caused people to scratch their heads.

Even at the plate, Berra defied logic. He swung at everything, yet he rarely struck out. Though he stood just five-feet eight-inches tall, he rapped .285 for his career while belting 358 home runs—an enormous total for a catcher. Defensively, "he springs on a bunt like it was another dollar," said manager Casey Stengel.[6] He also called pitches

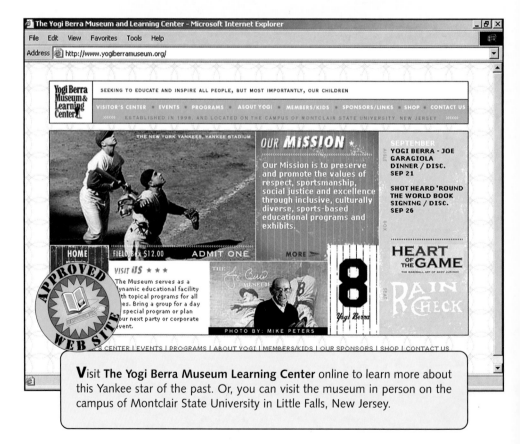

Visit **The Yogi Berra Museum Learning Center** online to learn more about this Yankee star of the past. Or, you can visit the museum in person on the campus of Montclair State University in Little Falls, New Jersey.

masterfully with his pitchers while purposefully distracting batters with "friendly" chitchat.

The end results: three AL MVP Awards, fifteen straight All-Star berths, fourteen pennants, and ten world titles. No other catcher in history has been as successful—or delightful—as the one and only Yogi Berra.

Mickey Mantle

A young baseball fan once told Detroit Tigers great Al Kaline, "You're not half as good as Mickey Mantle." Kaline replied, "Son, nobody is half as good as Mickey Mantle."[7]

In the book *The Best of Baseball,* writers rated Mantle among the ten strongest sluggers, ten fastest runners, and ten best bunters in baseball history. On April 17, 1953, he blasted the longest home run ever recorded: 565 feet.

A three-time AL MVP, "The Mick" in 1956 led the league in batting (.353), homers (52), and RBIs (130). He powered the Yankees to twelve AL pennants, and his eighteen World Series homers remain an all-time record.

In his eighteen years with the Yankees, Mantle crushed 536 home runs. All the while, he played on a chronically bad knee. Said Nellie Fox of the Chicago White Sox, "On two legs, Mickey Mantle would have been the greatest ballplayer who ever lived."[8]

▲ *The Mick was one of the most physically gifted baseball players fans of the sport ever saw. Although he was limited by injuries for much of his career, he put up incredible Hall of Fame statistics.*

Mantle is such an icon that his 1952 Topps baseball card has sold for $250,000. No other card from the last seventy years is worth more.

Whitey Ford

Off the field, Ford charmed visitors with a rosy-cheeked smile. But, said Mickey Mantle, "Stick a baseball in his hand and he became the most arrogant guy in the world."[9]

This crafty left-hander refused to lose. In fact, his .690 career winning percentage (236 wins, 106 losses) is a twentieth-century major-league record. Ford went 25–4 in 1961 and 24–7 in 1963.

Known as the "Chairman of the Board," Whitey excelled when the stakes were high. "If you had one game to win and your life depended on it," said Yankees manager Casey Stengel, "you'd want him to pitch it."[10]

Ford played on eleven pennant-winning Yankees teams and earned ten wins in the World Series—a record that still stands. Over one stretch, he pitched 32 consecutive scoreless innings in World Series play. In 1974, Ford—along with his good buddy Mantle—was inducted into the Baseball Hall of Fame.

Roger Maris

In 1961, as every Yankees fan knows, Roger Maris belted 61 home runs to break Babe Ruth's

Showing his fine pitching form, Whitey Ford gets ready to deliver the ball during this 1961 game. Ford excelled in the big games that mattered the most. He won more World Series games than any other pitcher.

major-league record. Yet, reflected Maris, "it would have been . . . a lot more fun if I had not hit those 61 home runs."[11]

Many fans and reporters did not want Maris to "tarnish" the legacy of the fabled Ruth. Others rooted for longtime Yankees hero Mickey Mantle to break Ruth's record instead (he hit 54 homers in 1961). Maris was so worn down by the pressure and negative publicity that he skipped a late-season game to go shopping with his wife.

Maris actually was a terrific all-around player. He shone in the outfield and on the base paths, and he played with a fierce determination. He won the AL MVP Award with New York in 1960 (39 homers, 112 RBIs) as well as in 1961.

Tragically, injuries and health problems cut short his career and his life. Maris died of cancer at age fifty-one in 1985. His home run record survived all the way to 1998. When Mark

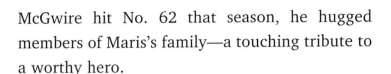

McGwire hit No. 62 that season, he hugged members of Maris's family—a touching tribute to a worthy hero.

Reggie Jackson

"If I played in New York," Reggie Jackson mused while with the Oakland A's, "they'd name a candy bar after me."[12] Jackson joined the Yankees in 1977, and a year later he bit into his first Reggie Bar.

A charismatic slugger, Jackson dominated headlines in New York. Manager Billy Martin despised Reggie's large ego, but everyone loved

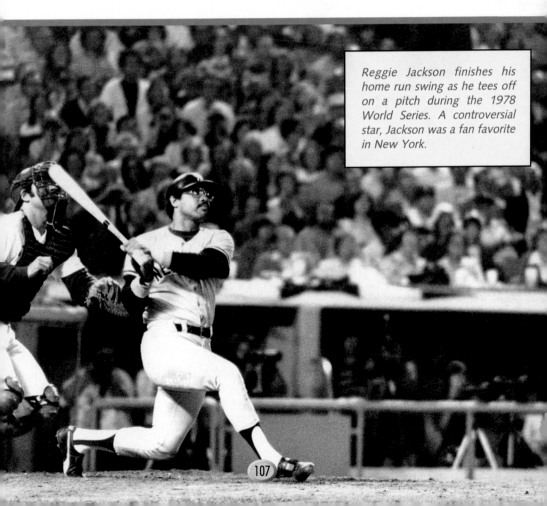

Reggie Jackson finishes his home run swing as he tees off on a pitch during the 1978 World Series. A controversial star, Jackson was a fan favorite in New York.

his home runs. He belted 32 four-baggers in 1977 and five more in that year's World Series. His three straight longballs in the title-clinching Game 6 earned him the nickname "Mr. October."

Jackson powered New York's drive to the 1978 world title as well, driving in 8 runs in the World Series. In 1980, he rapped .300 with 41 home runs for the Bombers.

Though Jackson played just five seasons in New York, he brought championship glory back to Yankee Stadium. A modern Babe Ruth, he compensated for strikeouts and controversy with home runs and winning hits. In 1993, the Yankees retired his No. 44.

→ Don Mattingly

Dwight Gooden was among the many pitchers who feared the wrath of Don Mattingly. "He has that look that few hitters have," Gooden said. "I

Former Yankees captain Don Mattingly was known as Donnie Baseball. In 2006, he served as the Yankees hitting coach, and was named bench coach for the 2007 season.

don't know if it's his stance, his eyes, or what, but you can tell he means business."[13]

During the "dark ages" of Yankees baseball—the 1980s—Mattingly shone bright. At first base, he won nine Gold Gloves and tied the MLB record for the highest career fielding percentage (.996). Batting out of a crouched stance, he rang line drives all over the yard.

After cracking .343 in 1984, Donnie Baseball won the AL MVP Award in 1985 thanks to 145 RBIs. A year later, he ripped .352 with 53 doubles. In 1987, he tied a major-league record by homering in eight straight games. He also smashed 6 grand slams that year—a new MLB record.

Back problems cut short his career, yet the Yankees made sure Mattingly would never be forgotten. In 1997, they retired his No. 23.

Derek Jeter

From childhood on, all Derek Jeter wanted to do was play shortstop for the New York Yankees. In 1995, his dream came true. He beamed, "I hope I wear this jersey forever."[14]

Immediately, Jeter energized the Yankees. His bat, speed, glove, and spirit earned him the 1996 AL Rookie of the Year Award. With Jeter as a catalyst, the Yankees roared to world titles in 1996, 1998, 1999, and 2000. With his good looks

▲ *Derek Jeter (left) and Mariano Rivera (right) are two modern Yankees stars who led the team's resurgence in the late 1990s.*

and winning smile, he became New York's "most eligible bachelor."

In his first ten seasons, Jeter reached 100 runs nine times, .300 seven times, 20 homers three times, and 30 steals twice. He won two Gold Gloves, and twice he earned MVP honors at the All-Star Game.

Nearly every year, Jeter has thrived in post-season play. "[T]he tougher the situation," said manager Joe Torre, "the more fire he gets in his eyes."[15]

The proof is in the numbers. Through 2006, Jeter's 150 hits in postseason play were the most in major-league history.

Mariano Rivera

For more than a decade, the Yankees have been the best team in baseball at preserving late-inning leads. Their secret: a composed Panamanian relief pitcher named Mariano Rivera.

Former Yankees closer Rich Gossage said that when Rivera takes the mound, the other team "is sitting in the dugout thinking, 'We've got no chance. It's over.' This guy walks into the game, and they are done."[16]

With his slight frame and easy motion, Rivera appears anything but intimidating. Yet he fires the best "cut fastball" in the game—a 95-mph blazer with a sharp break. From 1997 to 2005, Rivera averaged 42 saves per season. Three times he led the AL in saves (with a high of 53), and six times he posted ERAs below 2.00.

In postseason play, Rivera ranks as the most successful reliever ever. In 73 playoff and World Series games from 1995 to 2006, he logged 34 saves and a 0.80 ERA. Over one stretch, he tossed a record 33 1/3 consecutive scoreless innings in

▲ Current Yankees star Alex Rodriguez is surely a future Hall of Famer. He won the 2005 AL MVP as a member of the Yankees.

the postseason. Said Alex Rodriguez, "He has been the heart and soul of the New York Yankees dynasty."[17]

Alex Rodriguez

When the Texas Rangers traded Alex Rodriguez to the Yankees in 2004, A-Rod realized he could not wear his No. 3 uniform in New York. That was Babe Ruth's number, and it was retired. Rodriguez settled for No. 13, but he proceeded to put up Ruth-like statistics.

After ten seasons as a shortstop for Seattle and Texas, Rodriguez moved to third base with the Yankees. In 2004, he belted "only" 36 home runs, ending his amazing streak of six straight 40-homer seasons. But in 2005, he assured his spot in Yankee lore while en route to the AL MVP Award.

Rodriguez in 2005 ranked second in the AL in batting (.321) and became the first Yankee to win the league home run title since Reggie Jackson. His 48 homers broke Joe DiMaggio's team record for a right-handed batter. On April 26, he crushed 3 big flys and drove in 10 runs in one game.

A-Rod also smashed his 400th home run in 2005, becoming at age twenty-nine the youngest player ever to do so. Health permitting, he might someday surpass Babe Ruth's total of 714 home runs—and perhaps become baseball's home-run king.

Report Links

The Internet sites described below can be accessed at http://www.myreportlinks.com

▶**New York Yankees Official Site**
Editor's Choice Visit this official site for news of the team.

▶**National Baseball Hall of Fame and Museum**
Editor's Choice Visit this museum site to learn more about the game of baseball.

▶**Major League Baseball Players Association**
Editor's Choice Check on your favorite player here.

▶**BabeRuth.com**
Editor's Choice This is the official Web site of the Sultan of Swing.

▶**"'The Boss' Made Yankees a Dictatorship"**
Editor's Choice This article provides a look at the infamous George Steinbrenner.

▶**Baseball**
Editor's Choice This PBS site takes a look at the story of baseball.

▶***Baseball Almanac:* New York Yankees**
A short overview of Yankee history.

▶**CBS Sportsline: New York Yankees**
This CBS Sports site provides an in-depth look at the New York Yankees.

▶**A 'Curse' Born of Hate**
This article details the rivalry between the Yankees and the Red Sox.

▶**Digital Ballparks: New York Yankees**
Take virtual tours of baseball's greatest stadiums when you visit this Web site.

▶**Dressed to the Nines**
This is a history of the baseball uniform.

▶**The Greatest Team: 1927 Yankees**
Learn more about one of the greatest baseball teams in history.

▶**A History of Champions**
A nice overview of Yankee history.

▶**Mel Allen**
A biography of Yankees broadcaster Mel Allen.

▶**New York Yankees Clubhouse**
Visit this ESPN site for the New York Yankees.

Report Links

The Internet sites described below can be accessed at http://www.myreportlinks.com

▶**The New York Yankees Greatest Hits**
This *Sports Illustrated* Web site focuses in on some of the Yankees' best moments.

▶**New York Yankees Managers**
This site provides an overview on each New York Yankee manager.

▶**New York Yankees (1903–Present)**
A historical overview of the Yankees.

▶**The Official Site of Casey Stengel**
Take an online tour of Casey Stengel's life.

▶**The Official Site of Joe DiMaggio**
Find out more about Joltin' Joe from this Web site.

▶**The Official Web Site of Lou Gehrig**
Read about Lou Gehrig when you visit this site.

▶**Salaries Database**
Check major league ballplayer salaries on this Web site.

▶**Science of Baseball**
The Exploratorium science museum explores the science of baseball.

▶**Society for American Baseball Research (SABR)**
SABR is dedicated to the study of baseball.

▶**Torre's Run in NYC Includes Great Memories**
This Fox Sports article takes a look at Joe Torre.

▶**2001 World Series**
The New York Yankees play ball after the tragedy of 9/11.

▶**2003 World Series: Baseball-Reference.com**
The 2003 World Series is highlighted on this site.

▶**Yankee Stadium**
This site has facts, figures, and photos about Yankee Stadium.

▶**Yankee Stadium/New York Yankees**
This is an overview of Yankee Stadium.

▶**The Yogi Berra Museum and Learning Center**
This site highlights the life and career of Yogi Berra.

Career

MVP AWARD WINNERS*	YEAR	AVG	HR	RBI
Babe Ruth	1923	.393	41	131
Lou Gehrig	1927	.373	47	175
Lou Gehrig	1936	.354	49	152
Joe DiMaggio	1939	.381	30	126
Joe DiMaggio	1941	.357	30	125
Joe Gordon	1942	.322	18	103
Spud Chandler	1943	Pitcher, 20–4, 1.64 ERA		
Joe DiMaggio	1947	.315	20	97
Phil Rizzuto	1950	.324	7	66
Yogi Berra	1951	.294	27	88
Yogi Berra	1954	.307	22	125
Yogi Berra	1955	.272	27	108
Mickey Mantle	1956	.353	52	130
Mickey Mantle	1957	.365	34	94
Roger Maris	1960	.283	39	112
Roger Maris	1961	.269	61	142
Mickey Mantle	1962	.321	30	89
Elston Howard	1963	.287	28	85
Thurman Munson	1976	.302	17	105
Don Mattingly	1985	.324	35	145
Alex Rodriguez	2005	.321	48	130

*MVP Award was known as the League Award from 1922–29

CY YOUNG AWARD WINNERS*	YEAR	W	L	ERA
Bob Turley	1958	21	7	2.97
Whitey Ford	1961	25	4	3.21
Sparky Lyle	1977	13	5	2.17
Ron Guidry	1978	25	3	1.74
Roger Clemens	2001	20	3	3.51

*Cy Young Award first presented in 1956

Stats

PLAYER	YRS	G	AB	R	H	HR	RBI	SB	AVG
Yogi Berra	19	2,120	7,555	1,175	2,150	358	1,430	30	.285
Earle Combs	12	1,455	5,746	1,186	1,866	58	632	96	.325
Joe DiMaggio	13	1,736	6,821	1,390	2,214	361	1,537	30	.325
Lou Gehrig	17	2,164	8,001	1,888	2,721	493	1,995	102	.340
Elston Howard	14	1,605	5,363	619	1,471	167	762	9	.274
Reggie Jackson	21	2,820	9,864	1,551	2,584	563	1,702	228	.262
Derek Jeter	12	1,679	6,790	1,277	2,150	183	860	249	.317
Tony Lazzeri	14	1,740	6,297	986	1,840	178	1,191	148	.292
Mickey Mantle	18	2,401	8,102	1,677	2,415	536	1,509	153	.298
Roger Maris	12	1,463	5,101	826	1,325	275	851	21	.260
Don Mattingly	14	1,785	7,003	1,007	2,153	222	1,099	14	.307
Thurman Munson	11	1,423	5,344	696	1,558	113	701	48	.292
Phil Rizzuto	13	1,661	5,816	877	1,588	38	563	149	.273
Alex Rodriguez	13	1,746	6,767	1,358	2,067	464	1,347	241	.305
Babe Ruth	22	2,503	8,399	2,174	2,873	714	2,213	123	.342

PLAYER	YRS	G	IP	W	L	SV	SO	SHO	ERA
Roger Clemens	23	691	4,817.7	348	178	0	4,604	46	3.10
Whitey Ford	16	498	3,170.3	236	106	10	1,956	45	2.75
Ron Guidry	14	368	2,392.0	170	91	4	1,778	26	3.29
Waite Hoyt	21	674	3,762.3	237	182	52	1,206	26	3.59
Sparky Lyle	16	899	1,390.3	99	76	238	873	0	2.88
Andy Pettitte	12	367	2,312.3	186	104	0	1,703	4	3.81
Mariano Rivera	12	720	881.7	59	40	413	783	0	2.29

Career stats include all teams these athletes played for through 2006.

American League—One of baseball's two major leagues; the other is the National League.

amyotrophic lateral sclerosis—A fatal disease that attacks a person's motor skills and leads to increasing muscular weakness. It is also called Lou Gehrig's Disease.

Bronx Bombers—A nickname for the New York Yankees baseball team given to them because they play in the Bronx borough of New York City.

"called shot"—When a player points to where he intends to hit the ball and then does it. Many think that Babe Ruth did this in the 1932 World Series.

Curse of the Bambino—A superstitious hex that many Boston Red Sox fans believe was put on the team as punishment for the franchise selling Babe Ruth to the Yankees.

Death Valley—A nickname given to left-center field at Yankee Stadium. Fly balls just seem to die out there, making it difficult to hit home runs to that part of the ballpark.

dinger—Another word for a home run.

Division Series—A best-of-five series that determines who will play in the League Championship Series. The Division Series began in 1995.

fireballer—A pitcher known for throwing hard fastballs.

Five O'Clock Lightning—A nickname given to the 1927 Yankees, which featured perhaps the strongest lineup in baseball history.

Gold Glove—An annual award given to the best fielder at each position.

homer—Another word for a home run.

Javits Center—A convention center in the Manhattan borough of New York City.

Major League Baseball Players Association—A union that represents all of the baseball players in the major leagues.

Most Valuable Player—Annual award given to the player who the Baseball Writers Association of America (BBWAA) feel most helped his team succeed.

Murderers' Row—A nickname given to the batting order of the 1927 Yankees, which included big hitters Earle Combs, Lou Gehrig, Babe Ruth, Tony Lazzeri, and Bob Meusel.

no-hitter—A game in which a pitcher does not surrender a base hit.

PA man—The public address announcer.

pennant—A league championship decided by the winner of the League Championship Series.

perfect game—A game in which a pitcher does not allow the opposing team to reach base.

platoon—A situation where two players share playing time at a position.

round-tripper—Another term for a home run.

shutout—When a pitcher pitches a complete game without allowing a run.

sidearm pitcher—A pitcher who delivers the ball from his side rather than by throwing over the top.

skipper—Another word for a manager.

small-market team—A team that plays in a city with a small local population as compared to teams that play in or near larger cities.

Stengelese—A nickname used to describe the way Yankees manager Casey Stengel spoke.

Subway Series—An event that occurs when the two New York teams play each other in the World Series.

switch-hitter—A player who bats right-handed against left-handed pitchers and bats left-handed against right-handed pitchers.

three-peat—When a team wins three consecutive championships.

Triple Crown—A hitter wins the Triple Crown if he leads the league in home runs, runs batted in, and batting average all in the same season. There is also a pitcher's triple crown, which is achieved when a pitcher leads the league in wins, earned run average, and strikeouts all in the same season.

Chapter 1. Rising From the Ashes

1. Scott Lindlaw, "Bush throws out first pitch before Game 3," *USA Today* (Associated Press), October 31, 2001, <http://www.usatoday.com/sports/baseball/01play/2001-10-30-bush.htm> (December 16, 2005).

2. "Classic Clemens," *CNN/Sports Illustrated* (Associated Press), October 31, 2001, <http://sportsillustrated.cnn.com/baseball/mlb/2001/worldseries/news/2001/10/30/clemens_ap> (December 16, 2005).

3. Ian Browne, "Browne: Yankees create their own destiny," *MLB.com,* November 2, 2001, <http://www.mlb.com/NASApp/mlb/ws/news/ws_news_story.jsp?article=1122001-0324> (December 16, 2005).

Chapter 2. The Team That Ruth Built

1. Paul Adomites and Saul Wisnia, *Babe Ruth: His Life and Times* (Lincolnwood, Ill.: Publications International, 1995), p. 73.

2. Ibid., p. 94.

3. Ibid., p. 95.

4. "Ruth Crashes Out Homers 50 and 51," *The New York Times,* September 25, 1920, p. 19.

5. Lowell Reidenbaugh, *Baseball's 25 Greatest Teams* (St. Louis: The Sporting News, 1988), p. 9.

6. Ibid., p. 164.

7. "Full text version of the Farewell Speech," *Lou Gehrig: The Official Web Site,* n.d., <http://www.lougehrig.com/about/speech.htm> (December 8, 2005).

8. Dave Anderson, "The Longest Hitting Streak in History," *Sports Illustrated,* July 17, 1961, <http://sportsillustrated.cnn.com/baseball/mlb/features/1998/yankees/flashbacks/july61.html> (December 8, 2005).

Chapter 3. From Yogi to Reggie

1. Glenn Stout, *Yankees Century* (Boston: Houghton Mifflin, 2002), p. 200.

2. Paul Dickson, *Baseball's Greatest Quotations* (New York: HarperCollins Publishers, 1991), p. 44.

3. Paul Adomites et al., *The Golden Age of Baseball* (Lincolnwood, Ill.: Publications International, 2003), p. 130.

4. Ibid., p. 133.

5. Paul Adomites, Bobby Cassidy, Saul Wisnia, *Sluggers! History's Heaviest Hitters* (Lincolnwood, Ill.: Publications International, 1999), p. 46.

6. Lowell Reidenbaugh, *Baseball's 25 Greatest Teams* (St. Louis, The Sporting News, 1988), p. 144.

7. Joseph Reichler, *Baseball's Greatest Moments* (New York: Bonanza Books, 1984), p. 71.

8. "Quotations About Don Larsen," *Baseball Almanac,* n.d., <http://www.baseball-almanac.com/quotes/quolars .shtml> (December 18, 2005).

9. Lewis Early, "Mickey Quotes," *Mickey Mantle,* n.d., <http://www.themick.com/MickeyQuotes3.htm> (December 19, 2005).

10. Adomites, *The Golden Age of Baseball,* p. 195.

11. "Roger Maris Quotes," *BrainyQuote,* n.d., <http:// www.brainyquote.com/quotes/quotes/r/rogermaris139802. html> (December 20, 2005).

12. Dickson, p. 203.

Chapter 4. The New Dynasty

1. Tom Withers, "Calm, cool and collected Yankees win Game 3," *Athens Daily News* (Associated Press), n.d., <http://www.onlineathens.com/1998/102198/1021.s11calm .html> (December 22, 2005).

2. Michael Knisley, "History of the World Series — 1998," *The Sporting News,* n.d., <http://www.sportingnews .com/archives/worldseries/1998.html> (December 22, 2005).

3. Glenn Stout, *Yankees Century* (Boston: Houghton Mifflin, 2002), p. 435.

4. *Newsweek,* October 30, 2000, cover.

5. "David Ortiz postgame quotes," *MLB.com,* October 18, 2004, <http://mlb.mlb.com/NASApp/mlb/mlb/news/ mlb_news.jsp?ymd=20041018&content_id=898641&vkey =ds2004news&fext=.jsp> (December 23, 2005).

6. "Boston's blow out caps unequaled comeback," *ESPN.com,* October 20, 2004, <http://sports.espn.go .com/mlb/recap?gameId=241020110> (December 23, 2005).

Chapter 5. The Masterminds

1. Paul Adomites and Saul Wisnia, *Babe Ruth: His Life and Times* (Lincolnwood, Ill.: Publications International, 1995), p. 79.

2. "Miller Huggins," *National Baseball Hall of Fame,* n.d., <http://www.baseballhalloffame.org/hofers_and _honorees/hofer_bios/huggins_miller.htm> (December 11, 2005).

3. "Joe McCarthy," *BaseballLibrary.com,* n.d., <http:// www.baseballlibrary.com/baseballlibrary/ballplayers/M/ McCarthy_Joe.stm> (December 11, 2005).

4. David Pietrusza, Matthew Silverman, Michael Gershman, ed., *Baseball: The Biographical Encyclopedia* (New York: Total/Sports Illustrated, 2000), p. 16.

5. Lewis Early, "Mickey Quotes," *Mickey Mantle,* n.d., <http://www.themick.com/MickeyQuotes2.htm> (December 13, 2005).

6. "Quotes: About Casey," *CaseyStengel: The Official Site,* n.d., <http://www.caseystengel.com/quotes_about .htm> (December 13, 2005).

7. Ibid.

8. Glenn Stout, *Yankees Century* (Boston: Houghton Mifflin, 2002), p. 321.

9. Richard Lally, *Bombers: An Oral History of the New York Yankees* (New York: Crown: 2002), pp. 199–200.

Chapter 6. Welcome to Yankee Stadium

1. "JimF, Guest," *NYYFans.com,* April 3, 2000, <http:// forums.nyyfans.com/showthread.php?t=395> (December 26, 2005).

2. Paul Adomites and Saul Wisnia, *The Best of Baseball* (Lincolnwood, Ill.: Publications International, 1996), p. 138.

3. Stephen Borelli, "'Voice of God,' presides over Yankees," *USA Today,* October 25, 2000, <http://www .usatoday.com/sports/baseball/comment/sbcol15.htm> (December 27, 2005).

4. Wayne Coffey, "One hundred years of greatness," *New York Daily News,* April 15, 2003, <http://www .nydailynews.com/sports/baseball/story/75445p_69729c .html> (December 28, 2005).

5. Michael O'Keefe and T. J. Quinn, "Yanks losing at Money Ball," *New York Daily News,* December 4, 2005, <http://www.nydailynews.com/sports/story/371464p_316044c.html> (December 28, 2005).

6. Rachel Breitman, "Yankees Strike Out: Stadium Plan Blasted," *City Limits,* August 22, 2005, <http://www.citylimits.org/content/articles/weeklyView.cfm?articlenumber=1765> (December 28, 2005).

7. Governor Pataki, "Mayor Bloomberg and New York Yankees Announce Plans for Area Revitalization and New Stadium," *New York State,* June 15, 2005, <http://www.ny.gov/governor/press/05/june15_05-3.htm> (December 29, 2005).

8. T. J. Quinn, "New Ballpark's a Winner," *New York Daily News,* June 16, 2005, <http://www.nydailynews.com/ front/story/319513p-273178c.html> (December 29, 2005).

Chapter 7. The Heroes

1. "Quotes by Babe Ruth," *BabeRuth.com,* n.d., <http://www.baberuth.com/flash/about/quotes.html> (January 2, 2006).

2. Kevin Cowherd, "Bigger than Life," *BabeRuth.com,* n.d., <http://www.baberuth.com/flash/about/quotes.html> (January 2, 2006).

3. "Year by Year Leaders for Batting Average," *Baseball Almanac,* n.d., <www.baseball-almanac.com/hitting/hibavg3.shtml> (January 2, 2006).

4. Dennis Gaffney, "What Made DiMaggio a Great Player?" *PBS.org,* n.d., <http://www.pbs.org/wgbh/amex/dimaggio/sfeature/essay.html> (January 2, 2006).

5. "Yogi Berra Quotes," *RinkWorks,* n.d., <http://rinkworks.com/said/yogiberra.shtml> (January 4, 2006).

6. Paul Adomites, et al., *The Golden Age of Baseball* (Lincolnwood, Ill.: Publications International, 2003), p. 135.

7. "Mickey Mantle Tribute," *ESPN.com,* August 11, 2000, <http://espn.go.com/classic/mantletribute000813.html> (January 4, 2006).

8. "Quotes About Mickey Mantle," *Baseball Almanac,* n.d., <http://www.baseball-almanac.com/quotes/quomant.shtml> (January 4, 2006).

9. David Pietrusza, Matthew Silverman, and Michael Gershman ed., *Baseball: The Biographical Encyclopedia* (New York: Total/Sports Illustrated, 2000), p. 369.

10. Ibid.

11. "Roger Maris Quotes," *BrainyQuote,* n.d., <http://www.brainyquote.com/quotes/quotes/r/rogermaris139808.html> (January 8, 2006).

12. Bruce Lowitt, "Mr. October lives up to star billing," *St. Petersburg Times,* November 28, 1999, <http://www.sptimes.com/News/112899/Sports/Mr_October_lives_up_t.shtml> (January 8, 2006).

13. "Quotations About Don Mattingly," *Baseball Almanac,* n.d., <http://www.baseball-almanac.com/quotes/quomatt.shtml> (January 9, 2006).

14. "Derek Jeter," *Wikiquote,* n.d., <http://en.wikiquote.org/wiki/Derek_Jeter> (January 9, 2006).

15. Tom Verducci, "The Toast of the Town," *CNNSI.com,* November 6, 2000, <http://sportsillustrated.cnn.com/features/cover/news/2000/11/30/yankees_yir2/> (January 9, 2006).

16. Buster Olney, "The Confidence Man," *New York Magazine,* June 28, 2004, <http://newyorkmetro.com/nymetro/news/sports/features/9375/index1.html> (January 10, 2006).

17. "Quotes About Mariano Rivera," *Baseball Almanac,* n.d., <http://www.baseball-almanac.com/quotes/mariano_rivera_quotes.shtml> (January 10, 2006).

Anderson, Dave, ed. *The New York Yankees Illustrated History.* New York: St. Martin's Press, 2002.

Gentile, Derek. *The Complete New York Yankees: The Total Encyclopedia of the Team.* New York: Black Dog & Leventhal Publishers, 2004.

Grabowski, John F. *The New York Yankees.* San Diego, Calif.: Lucent Books, 2001.

Lally, Richard. *Bombers: An Oral History of the New York Yankees.* New York: Crown Publishing Group, 2002.

McGough, Matthew. *Bat Boy: My True Life Adventures Coming of Age with the New York Yankees.* New York: Doubleday Publishing, 2005.

The New York Times. *Sultans of Swat: The Four Great Sluggers of the New York Yankees.* New York: St. Martin's Press, 2006.

Robinson, Ray and Christopher Jennison. *Pennants and Pinstripes: The New York Yankees 1903–2002.* New York: Black Dog & Leventhal Publishers, Inc., 2001.

Stout, Glenn. *Yankees Century.* Boston: Houghton Mifflin, 2002.

Vancil, Mark and Mark Mandrake, eds. *The New York Yankees: One Hundred Years.* New York: Ballantine Books, 2003.

Vancil, Mark and Mark Mandrake. *The Greatest Yankees Teams.* New York: Ballantine Books, 2004.